Walking to Emmaus

Walking to Emmaus

EAMON DUFFY

BURNS & OATES
A Continuum imprint
LONDON • NEW YORK

Burns & Oates
The Tower Building, 11 York Road, London SE1 7NX
80 Maiden Lane, Suite 704, New York, NY 10038

www.continuumbooks.com

First published 2006

British Library Cataloguing-in-Publication Data
A catalogue record for this book is available from the British Library.

ISBN 0 8601 2423 1

Typeset by YHT Ltd, London
Printed and bound by Antony Rowe Ltd.

Contents

For Ronald Hyam

Introduction

A book of sermons by a Roman Catholic layman is something of an anomaly. The modern Catholic Church discourages lay preaching, and forbids it altogether at the Eucharist. A dear (and now deceased) friend, who happened also to be a Roman Catholic bishop, once invited me to speak at his annual diocesan pilgrimage. He was deluged with agitated correspondence from zealously orthodox lay-people, scandalized by advance publicity announcing that a lay academic was to deliver a 'sermon' on the occasion. 'Sermon' was duly emended to 'address' and all, in the end, was well.

The sermons and addresses gathered here were, however, mostly delivered in non-denominational university settings – in the Chapel of my own and of other Cambridge Colleges, and in the University pulpits of Oxford and Cambridge. Two dozen Cambridge Colleges support a Chapel which uses Anglican forms of worship, but attracts an eclectic congregation of many denominations and none. In most of those Chapels the best-attended

Sunday service is Choral Evensong, a service of psalms, hymns and anthems, with two substantial Bible readings, and an expository sermon. So Sunday by Sunday, for twenty weeks of the year, two dozen College Chaplains must find two dozen preachers to meet the need. As a result, anyone who teaches theology within the University, lay or clerical, Catholic or Protestant, is liable to be pressed into service: and anyone unwise enough to agree more than once is liable to be targeted often. This book is the result.

Preaching in a College Chapel is an exercise significantly different from that of preaching in a parish church. A University sermon is, of course, addressed to a congregation used to sustained attention to argument and exposition, and who are critical by inclination, instinct and training. They are liable to judge a sermon not only on its coherence and instructional content, but also on its entertainment value. This can be daunting. Equally daunting is the fact that though some of one's listeners are likely to possess an informed Christian faith and a regular Church allegiance, others will be uninstructed and uncommitted, seekers after truth, the merely curious, or there mainly for the music. Meeting the needs and expectations of such different constituencies in a single utterance can tax the preacher's integrity as well as his intelligence. These sermons are all, in one way or another, Christian reflections on the central affirmations of the Christian faith, but they were addressed in most cases to congregations which included many who would not describe themselves as Christians. It is my hope that readers in the same position may find something here that speaks to them, as well as to the more committed.

Anglican Choral Evensong is to my mind the greatest liturgical achievement of the Reformation, a perfect blend of noble prayer in memorable language set to glorious music. At its heart is the reading of two extended passages of Scripture, one each from the Old and New Testaments. The preacher's task is to help the congregation to hear the words of Scripture, addressed to them not as an abstract exercise in exegesis, but as a word of life addressed to their own particular situation. So although I am a professional historian and not a biblical exegete, most of these sermons involve the close reading of a biblical passage. To get the best from them, the reader will need to have a Bible handy, and to read beforehand the passages which the sermons seek to expound. And if these utterances do no more than send their readers back to the original biblical passages, then they will have done a little good.

Eamon Duffy
Magdalene College
Cambridge

1

Among the tombs

Magdalene College, Cambridge
Readings: Isa. 65:1–5; Mk 5

The wonderful cluster of stories in chapter five of the Gospel of St Mark is shot through with some of his most characteristic emphases – they are hardly pre-dinner fare: violence, madness, unclean spirits, isolation, disease, and death.

Above all, isolation – the madman who dwells alone among the tombs, the woman put beyond the pale by a vile disease, the dead girl in the stillness of an inner room, while outside hired mourners pipe and wail.

In every one of these stories, Jesus and the other central characters are alone, even though they are surrounded by crowds, pressed in on and hindered from movement. The demoniac man is actually invaded by a crowd of unclean spirits, whose name is Legion, and whose presence is the sign of a disintegrated and self-destructive personality, a divided mind. And all this takes place, as we are several times reminded, by the side of the sea, whose turbulence Christ has just stilled, in the verses immediately before our reading, when it threatens to smother the apostles in their boat, just as it will smother the pigs and the demons who possess them. For the Jews, the sea was always to be feared, the symbol of chaos, noisy, threatening, *turbulent*; and *turba* is in fact the Latin word used again and again for the crowds in the Vulgate version of these stories, recurring like the clanging of a bell. For Mark, the crowds and the sea are the same: the human as well as the natural environment threatens to overwhelm and drown the characters of his story.

Mark's view of human existence is grim: his Gospel begins with the cry of the gaunt and enigmatic prophet John, a voice crying in the wilderness – and it ends with a group of bewildered women, fleeing in terror and bafflement from the mystery of the empty sepulchre. For Mark, the Gospel, like human life itself, begins with a cry and ends with a tomb, and in between is the noise and turbulence of the sea.

These stories have always made people uncomfortable. Take the Gadarene swine, for example: the story is full of magic, for all that business about names – the demons calling out Jesus's name before 'adjuring' him not to torment them; and then Jesus demanding the demons' name, and then the demons giving a number instead of a name – all that is in fact part and parcel of first-century belief about exorcism and magic: you needed to have someone's name to have power over them, and this shouting match about names is actually a struggle for domination.

Then there are the pigs themselves: two thousand of them stampeded to death by the demons, apparently with

Jesus's permission. The owners of the herds in the story are frightened, aggrieved and alienated, and some readers have shared their feelings ever since. Whether you are an animal-lover (all those poor little piggies), or a defender of property (all that marketable livestock, which someone had to pay for), the story is shocking. Bertrand Russell liked to say that this story was one good reason why no decent man, such as himself I suppose, could be a Christian. But it was not just militant atheists who got on their high horse about it (if I can change animals for a minute): liberal Protestant commentators have spent anguished hours thinking up excuses and explanations. The favourite one is that there were of course no demons: that was only the early Church's primitive, pre-scientific world-view: actually the man was deranged, maybe a schizophrenic, and his cure by Jesus (which, because it is the cure of *mental* illness, is somehow supposed to be less miraculous than casting out the demons) was marked by a violent seizure, which scared the daylights out of the grazing herd, and sent them lemming-like into the sea. Nobody's fault after all, just one of those things; for how could the beloved teacher be so cruel, or so careless of other people's property?

Other commentators have been tougher minded. All this worry about the pigs, they say, is beside the point, for this story never actually happened. It is in fact a legend about some other rabbi, a grim Jewish joke, in which the sort of people who eat ham sandwiches get their come uppance, and serve them right; or, in Isaiah's grander language, a people 'which remain among the graves, and lodge in the monuments, which eat swine's flesh, and broth of abominable things is in their vessels.' Demons are filthy things, but then pork is too, so naturally they belong together. Where else would devils go when forced to leave their pagan victim? And anyway, the cream of the joke is on the demons, because instead of a comfortable alternative lodging in the pigs, they end up, in Mark's vivid phrase, choked in the sea. According to this theory, the whole story was taken up from Jewish folklore by the early Christians, and adapted to demonstrate Christ's power.

And then there is the miracle of the woman with the menstrual haemorrhage, ritually unclean and a social outcast because of it, who thinks that just touching the tassels which Jesus, as an Orthodox Jew, wore on the corners of his robe, will magically heal her illness: what she is doing is terrible, for her touch will pollute Jesus, as it will all who brush against her in that seething crowd. So, in her desperation, she tries to steal power from Christ, and she succeeds. And he feels it go, yet at first he clearly doesn't know who has taken it – he only identifies her because she is trapped by the crowd, and she falls down before him, and confesses all.

Finally, there is the ambiguous story of the little girl, the daughter, not of a pagan or an outcast, but of a Jewish religious leader, who is nevertheless reduced by the fact of mortality to being a beggar at Jesus' door. But what is going on: is the little girl dead at all? In Matthew's and Luke's versions of this miracle, there is no doubt about it, she is raised from the dead; but here the Lord seems to

deny it – once more, Mark seems more interested in the
contrast between the clamour of the crowd and the silence
which Jesus insists on creating around the little girl than in
the precise character of the miracle. And the same commentators who try to explain away the demons at Gadara
have seized on this ambiguity – the girl is raised not from
the dead, but from a diabetic coma, as if the Lord had not
called her from the sleep of death, but only slipped her a
candy bar or a couple of sugar lumps.

Demons, ritual uncleaness, Jewish funerals. What is all
this about? Where is there anything in it for people like us,
who never encounter demons and reject the very notion
of ritual uncleaness; for whom madness and disease are
scientifically explicable; who do not believe in, or at any
rate do not expect to see, resurrections from the dead, nor
indeed any other miracles?

The people in these stories are, quite literally, falling
apart – their personalities disintegrated, like the demoniac,
and turned in violence on themselves. The only order is
the one imposed, unsuccesfully, by force and broken
chains. Or like the woman, they are thrust apart from
other human beings by a disease which human effort only
makes worse, bled dry not only by her illness but by the
bogus experts who claim the power to heal; or like the
little girl, locked away from everyone in a death portrayed
as a sleep, but not the sleep of peace – instead, it is an
uneasy sleep, troubled by the tumult and the angry
laughter of the crowd.

'Stand by thyself, come not near to me,' say the people
who dwell among the tombs in the passage we heard read

from Isaiah, and which Mark had in mind when he compiled these stories. In each of them, human society before Christ's intervention shuns or crushes the individual. When, in the tumult on his way to Jairus's house, Jesus looks round and asks who the woman is who has touched him, the disciples are openly scornful – in such a crowd, they demand, how can *anyone* be known: 'Thou seest the multitude thronging thee, and sayest thou, who touched me?' The people in these stories don't relate, they move aggressively or furtively – they run at Jesus, like the demoniac; they throng him; or like the woman they creep up behind, hoping to escape again, unseen. No-one communicates with anyone: the demoniac has no speech but a cry or the deceitful aggressive voices of the demons; the woman with the haemorrhage speaks, but only to herself; the crowds wail or, like the disciples, laugh in scorn.

Mark is not writing about the especially desperate situation in first-century Gallilee, which he almost certainly did not know: it is the *world* he is describing, our world, a world without God. In these opening years of the third millenium we feel with a new intensity the depth of this human alienation from the presence of God and from each other. With the help of television we feast each night on horrors – starvation and the aftermath of war in Afghanistan and Iraq, conflict and terror in Israel, private crime and public atrocity, and, maybe worse than all, the collapse of shared value, the new certainty that there can be no certainties, that we invent morality as we invent taste, that there lies before us not the will of God for human flourishing, but the supermarket of values, where everything is for grabs – no right, no wrong, no true, no false, just my choice and your choice. And if we are conservative we call for a stronger police-force and tougher laws, hoping by coercion to control forces which no man can bind, no, not with chains; and if we are liberals we preen ourselves on all this bewilderment, and call it pluralism, or, if we work in the University, perhaps, post-modernism, and think of ourselves as enlightened; but Mark's name for it was Legion, and he saw that it is tearing us apart.

Into this disintegrating horror comes the figure of Jesus, armed with authority and power. Mark believed, and wants us to believe, that this was no mere man, but the finger of the living God: we are in the presence of miracle. But see what the miracles achieve: not the extraordinary, the occult, but the restoration of what is truly normal. The man divided by a thousand unclean spirits is restored, not merely to himself – clothed, and in his right mind – but to human companionship. He wants to leave everything and follow Jesus, but Jesus forbids it: he is not to return to isolation, nor to the crowds, but to his family and friends, to true, normal, real, community. Mark is far more insistent on this element of the restoration of human ordinariness in the healing than the other evangelists, and it emerges again in the story of Jairus' daughter: the crowd, the sign of tumult, disorder and disintegration, is banished; the witnesses are to be the closest disciples and her family, and it is to her family, and to the sharing of a meal, that she is restored.

The miracle of Christ's healing power in these stories is to restore us to our right minds, to make us feel, in our bodies, like the woman healed of the haemorrhage, that we are as we ought to be, to see the world aright like the healed demoniac; above all, to give us back to one another. In the midst of the frenzy of the demons, or the directionless turbulence of the crowd, and despite the dissolving power of disease and death, Jesus establishes a still point, a space in which human beings can speak to one another, and be what they are meant to be – able to tell right from wrong, health from sickness, truth from lies – in fact, ordinary, sane, together. We have never needed that space more.

The blind demonic forces at work in these three stories are at work still in our world: each of us has had or will have experience of them. We must all die, or worse, watch our loved ones die; we must all suffer and eventually succumb to disease; some of us will experience in mental illness the dissolution of our personalities or the personalities of parents, family, friends, lovers. It looks, too, as if we are doomed to watch our society dissolve into the unmeaning turbulence of the crowd, as the rational and compassionate framework of a caring Christian society is eroded further and further, whichever government is in power, in the name of freedom of choice, and our common life is brought increasingly under the tyranny of the market, and of the masters – or is it slaves? – of the market, whose name also is Legion.

This is indeed a vision to dizzy and appal: but we should not be afraid. When Jesus raised Jairus' daughter, he banished all witnesses but Peter, James and John. They were to be alone with him twice more – on the mountain of transfiguration, and in the garden of Gethsemane. That double witness is a sign that Jesus, too, experienced these destructive forces, not just, as in these three stories, triumphantly, in the barely veiled power of his Godhead, but as a sufferer, in that longer and more terrible journey through the frenzy of the crowd, to Calvary. He too was an outcast, shunned even by his friends, He too was bound and left alone among the tombs. Yet it is our belief as Christians that the victory displayed in these miracle stories is only a pale shadow of the real victory he achieved in his dying. In that death, desolate and alone, he encountered and overcame all the forces that empty our existence of meaning, shape and companionship. Because of that death, our living and dying have meaning and hope.

We need to seize that hope, to live by it. It does not mean that life will hurt us less: hope is not an anaesthetic or a vague emotion, a sweetener of life's bitter pill; it is a call to action. It means living purposefully in the knowledge that life is not meaningless, or a journey alone towards oblivion. It is the knowledge that God has a destiny and a will for us, and that we can know it and do it, for he has revealed it in his Word and in his Church. In that Word he has lit a candle in the dark, a light for our steps. In that Church he has created a space in which we can be human together, and 'publish the great things that the Lord has done for us', so that men and women may 'marvel', and, marvelling, believe on His name.

2

Let Us Now Praise Famous Men

The Lady Margaret Sermon for the Commemoration of
the Benefactors of the University of Cambridge, 1992
Ecclesiasticus 44 1–15

Universities are curious, contrary places, and Oxford and
Cambridge more curious and contrary than most. At one
level they are centres of intellectual innovation and
advance, places where the atom is split, new wonder-
drugs developed, old orthodoxies overturned. And yet,
they are also the most conservative of institutions, wed-
ded, with a fidelity which our society hardly grants to any
ordinary marriage, to extraordinary rituals and ways of
doing things, whose sole commendation seems to be that
it has always been so. The contradiction is perhaps more
apparent than real; a strong sense of tradition is often a
help, not a hindrance, to intellectual openness. But it is
not always easy to see how that works in practice, and
much that we do and value in the ritual side of our
common life has, to an unsympathetic eye, a faint air of
the ridiculous about it. Today's service is a case in point.
Just what is all this about? Some of you may know the
spoof Commemoration Day address given by a lunatic
clergyman at the beginning of W.H. Auden's *The Orators:*

Commemoration: Commemoration. What *does* it mean? What does it mean? Not, what did it mean to them, there, then, but what does it mean to us, here, now? It's a *facer*, isn't it boys? But we've all got to answer it. What were the dead like? What sort of people are we living with now? Why are we here? What are we going to do?

In the Lady Margaret's day, the questions, 'why are we here, what are we going to do?', had a universally understood and straightforward answer. We are here to repay the kindness of our benefactors, by praying for the release of their souls from whatever torment they might be undergoing in purgatory. Chaucer's Clerk of Oxenford, of course, is the archetype:

> But al he myghte of his frendes hente
> On bookes and on learning he it spente,
> And bisily gan for the soules praye
> Of hem that yaf hym wherwith to scoleye.

In fact, that was the main motive for most of the founding benefactions of the University. Certainly it was the one behind the largesse of the Lady Margaret and her chaplain John Fisher, the effective founders of the modern University of Cambridge. The Colleges were first and foremost chantries. The return which benefactors expected from their largesse was the much needed prayers of celibate scholars, many of them engaged in the study of theology. Between the poor scholars and the rich givers there was a reciprocity of need, for the rich had it on the highest authority that they would enter heaven, if at all, only with extreme difficulty, a manoeuvre in fact as unlikely as squeezing a camel through a needle's eye. Any help afforded by the prayers of those whose studies and mode of life kept them close to heaven was gratefully received, and worth paying for.

But of course it has been some centuries since the original religious explanation of these curious occasions has been acceptable in the University: the Church of England, and its Universities, stopped praying for the dead in the reign of Edward VI, and whatever reciprocal reward our benefactors since then have hoped for, it has not been the help of our prayers.

Perhaps it is our praise they wanted. On the face of it that is the explanation of the traditional reading for these occasions: we have come to praise the powerful, the rich, the famous, above all the lavish givers:

Let us now praise famous men, and our fathers that begat us. Such as did bear rule in their kingdoms, men renowned for their power, rich men, furnished with ability. All these were honoured in their generations, and were the glory of their times. The people will tell of their wisdom, and the congregation will shew forth their praise.

In a few minutes the Vice-Chancellor will tell us who these famous men are whose praise we are to tell forth. And sure enough, it seems at first sight that they are a

selection of the mighty of the earth – Richard III; Henry
VIII, who came within a whisker of closing the whole
University down in the 1540s; George I, whose bene-
faction to the library was almost universally recognized at
the time as not really designed to promote learning, our
enterprise, but to reward political subservience, which of
course was his. At the same time that the Crown sent us
the books which form the core of the University Library,
it quartered a regiment of Cavalry to put down Jacobite
sedition in Oxford. The contrast gave rise to some famous
mocking verses:

> The King, observing with judicious eyes
> The state of both his Universities,
> To one he sent a regiment: for why?
> That learned body wanted loyalty.
> To t'other he sent books, as well discerning
> How much that loyal body wanted learning.

Can that be it, then? Does the roll-call of kings and
queens, dukes and duchesses, lawyers, politicians and
millionaires, which we will shortly hear recited, constitute
the meaning of this occasion: a commemoration of the fact
that the University is part of the establishment, a canonization of the violent, the powerful and the very, very
rich who have shared their wealth – in many cases their
loot – with us and our predecessors? Today is All Saints'
Day: are these our Saints?

This is a disturbing thought, because it suggests that
what we are about is at one and the same time an exercise

in sanctified flattery and self-congratulation, and a devastatingly revealing act of self-definition. For to name the significant dead is always to offer an account of ourselves. In a recognisable sense, every human community, from the family to the nation, chooses its own ancestors, or at any rate, chooses those whom it will remember and publicly acknowledge. So the names we name today do tell us something about how we see ourselves. Make what you like of it, they include the name of hardly a single scholar. These be your Gods, O Israel.

This is not the bilious perception of a late twentieth-century lefty. In 1905 a Fellow and future Master of Magdalene, Arthur Benson, attended a University Sermon in this very church, and was deeply depressed by what it seemed to reveal about the University. Afterwards he confided to his diary his loathing of,

> The slow, blear-eyed panting procession of Heads ...
> the nearly empty church, the snoring Masters who,
> God knows, want improving quite as much or more
> than the pious undergraduates who come. The stupid
> conventionality and stuffiness of the whole thing ...
> the heavy respectability, the complacent security, the
> dull consciousness of rectitude in work and success.

This is strong stuff for a Victorian public school housemaster, the son of an Archbishop of Canterbury, and the author of the words of *Land of Hope and Glory*. Benson's indictment has an almost prophetic ring to it. But is it true? Well, it is certainly the case, that the carefully selected list of the fathers who begat us is conventional, even complacent. It contains no one awkward, no one who stood outside, much less up against the Establishment of his or her day. We might reasonably expect to find in even the shortest list of the founding fathers of this University the name of John Fisher, the greatest Cambridge scholar of his times and the instigator or promoter of so much that was creative in Cambridge in the sixteenth century, that most formative of all the centuries of our history. If anyone in our past brings together passionate commitment to the University and its institutions, profound scholarship and unchallengeable human integrity, it is he. But he is not in our list: instead we commemorate the king who killed him.

It is also true that, for much of the time, what we seem to be dedicated to as an institution is the production of Establishment fodder: powerful men and women like those to be named in our roll of honour. Our pupils depart in search of wealth and fame, to be politicians, eminent lawyers, marketing consultants, something ruthless in the City. Is this what we celebrate? Is this what we are about?

Certainly, in commemorating our benefactors and therefore our past today, we are celebrating ourselves; and it is true that there is an inescapable element of shabbiness about that celebration. To contemplate our own past is to be brought up hard against a good deal that is shameful. Like every human institution, the University is compromised by its past.

It has always been so: even our most saintly benefactors, like the Lady Margaret whose benefactions include this sermon, was a hardened and sometimes ruthless politician, dedicated in her prime to the single-minded, and not always scrupulous, promotion of the interests of her own family before all else. Our medieval forebears were no better than us. They too reverenced success, they too averted their eyes from the vices and motives of the great, they too went fishing for benefactions, and gave thanks when they had netted them. But there was built into the very structure of their commemoration a devastating irony, which undercut and subverted the flattery which they heaped on the great ones of the earth. To pray for the munificent dead was to pay tribute to their success, their wealth, their conspicuous generosity: it was a sanctified form of flattery. But before and beyond all that, it was a declaration that they needed prayer: it insisted that in the one thing necessary, the search for salvation, the moneyed great were not so very successful after all, and the very things that made them great – power, wealth, grandeur – weighed them down and hindered their human completeness. Within their thanksgiving was enshrined an assertion of absolute value, which weighed wealth and power and success against truth and humility and the desire to understand rather than to master the world, and found it wanting.

We do not have that structural irony to help prevent us bowing down before values which are in fact deeply inimical to the enterprise of scholarship. Since we have not gathered to pray for our benefactors, we do not in this service declare that the great who have given to us were sinners like us. We have no obvious way of symbolizing the perception that power, wealth and the rule of the market are not necessarily the essential driving force of all human excellence; or that here in this place we serve values which go deeper and take men and women further along the path to wisdom, towards true humanity.

But there is a redemptive irony here all the same. It is to be found in our reading from the book of Ecclesiasticus. Ecclesiasticus does indeed seem to invite us to praise the famous men and women whom the Vice-Chancellor is just about to name – King Richard, King Henry, King George, the Duke of Somerset and all the rest. In fact it does no such thing. The 'fathers who begat us' are not the founders of Colleges and Chairs, Lectureships and Libraries. They are the patriarchs and prophets of Israel, and if you read on beyond the point where we stopped today, you will find that there is a list of them, for six long chapters, from Enoch and Abraham to Ezekiel and Nehemiah. These are the models set before us. They *do* include kings and war-leaders and rich men, but, for the author, that is not what was significant about them. To see what is, we need to look elsewhere.

Most people will never have read that list in Ecclesiasticus, since it is not normally counted as part of the Old Testament, and is not even included in most Bibles. So most people's acquaintance with it runs no further than the 'Let us praise famous men' verses we heard earlier. But in fact there is a very similar list, almost certainly modelled on the one in Ecclesiasticus, in the New Testament. It is to be found in chapter eleven of Hebrews, and is the well-known passage about the great cloud of witnesses which surrounds us. The end of that list in Hebrews draws out and underlines the irony of *our* lesson: having recited the list of famous men, much the same list, it recalls that some, indeed, 'subdued kingdoms, wrought righteousness, obtained promises, waxed valiant in fight'. But many also 'were stoned, were sawn asunder, were tempted, were slain with the sword ... being destitute, afflicted, tormented, they wandered in deserts and mountains, in dens and caves of the earth (of whom the world was not worthy)'.

That New Testament list spells out what is implicit in the list in Ecclesiasticus: that the greatness for which men and women should be held in remembrance can be, perhaps usually is, costly; that they are to be remembered, not for their success, but for their persistence in a faith and a hope which marked them off from the world of the merely powerful, the merely successful. For the writers of both passages, the memory which constitutes the community, reminding them of their origins and recalling them to integrity, is not anodyne, offering reassurance and lulling them into Benson's detested heavy respectability, complacent security, the dull consciousness of rectitude in work and success.

It is something far more searching, something which places a question mark against conventional measurements of achievement, and explicitly contrasts true achievement with what the world counts worth. In that perspective, the lesson we heard acts not as a blanket endorsement of the values of the great and the good in our list, but as an invitation to measure them and ourselves against starker and more demanding criteria of greatness.

At the heart of Christianity and its most fundamental mode of worship lies an act of remembrance, the commemoration of a benefactor. That benefactor is as different as could be from the captains and the kings we remember today. In the Christian Eucharist, what is recalled is, precisely, a resounding worldly failure: the gruesome death, outside the city, of a man who ruled no kingdom, made no fortune, won no wars, and who failed to persuade the majority of his contemporaries that he had anything of value to say.

His gift was his own death, a death that did *not* take him to the centre of human achievement. When he came to the courts and councils of kings, it was not as a colleague or valued servant, heaped with orders and honours, but as a condemned criminal. When his message was presented in the Academy, the philosophers and men of letters yawned, and promised that they would hear some more, another day.

It is this man whose memory constitutes the community of his disciples and nourishes their life, and which long ago brought this University into existence. Week by week, his memory is recalled not to lull into a complacent sense of achieved success, but to challenge and unsettle. 'Why have you come to disturb us?' demands the Grand Inquisitor of the silent Christ in Dostoevsky's fable. The Grand Inquisitor there stands for all that today's celebration should *not* be – the alliance of those whose proper concern is the freedom of the hearts and minds of humanity with worldly power, and all the forces which erode the precarious freedoms of humanity in favour of a bestial security, human aspiration reduced to bread and circuses.

The greatest memorialist of the twentieth century was the Italian Jewish poet and novelist, Primo Levi, whose whole writing career issues out of the year and a half he spent in Auschwitz from 1944. At the heart of Levi's work was a desire to recall the men and women, good and bad, whom he had encountered there, and, in the unblinking but compassionate remembrance of what, in that extremity, they had been, to discover what it was to be a man. In the remembrance of their evil he discovered his own moral fragility; in the remembrance of the less frequent heroism or even simple decencies, he discovered what it was to hope. Of one such remembered figure, Lorenzo, he wrote:

> ... it was due to Lorenzo that I am alive today ... because he constantly reminded me ... by his plain and natural manner of being good, that there still existed a just world outside our own, not corrupt, not savage, extraneous to hatred and terror, something difficult to define, a remote possibility of good, for which it was worth surviving ... Thanks to Lorenzo, I managed not to forget that I myself was a man.

For Levi, such acts of remembrance, so central to his own integrity, were directly akin to the academic enterprise. He himself was a chemist, and he recalled how in Mussolini's Italy, as the common life of Italy was dissolved in manipulative rhetoric, and truth gave way to a sickening mixture of political dogma and brutal expediency, the pursuit of the hard realities of chemistry had a dignity and majesty: the elements of the periodic table became for him,

> ... the antidote to Fascism, because they were clear and distinct and verifiable at every step, and not a tissue of lies and emptiness, like the radio and newspapers.

Every human community needs to recall its beginnings, to memorialize the ancestors, to celebrate its achievements. But if that act of remembrance is to nourish rather than to stifle, it must have the capacity continually to subvert our complacencies, to upset the compromises we make and are forced to make with the world of the great and the good. It is quite right that we should celebrate the part this community of learning has played in the construction of the wider community. We do right to give thanks that sceptre and crown have been deflected, if only momentarily, from the pursuit of power and persuasion, to fund the activities of those whose concern is to tell the truth, so far as it can be known. But we need to beware of a selective commemoration, which edits out the tension and downright opposition which will always exist and should always exist between the commercial and loose political worlds – the world of expediency, pragmatism and rhetoric, and our world. And at a time in our history when the world of political expediency and the power of the market are being brought to bear with unprecedented force on the fundamental structures and objectives of the University, we have never needed a firmer sense of what it is we are about – we have never needed more urgently a sense of the complexity of our own past.

The builders of the old Cambridge Divinity School got this right. Around its first storey they set niches in which they enshrined the great figures of Cambridge theology – the fathers who begat us. In compiling that pedigree they deliberately rejected the temptation to construct a selective memory, to edit out the tensions and contradictions within the past that has made us. On either side of the main entrance they set images of Thomas Cranmer and of John Fisher, two men who had bitterly opposed each other for the sake of truth, and two men who gave their lives in obedience to the truth as they understood it. It is as good an image as any of what an academic commemoration should be. There is room for the kings, the cabinet ministers and the captains of industry – but only if there is room also for the valiant for truth who withstood them to the face. Honouring them, we can keep faith with ourselves, and with them all.

May their souls, and the souls of all the faithful departed, through the mercy of God, rest in peace.

3

When I remember, I am afraid

Remembrance Sunday, University Church, Oxford, 1998
Readings: Job 21:6

Today is Remembrance Sunday. For two or three weeks
politicians, businessmen and media personalities have been
careful to wear a poppy, prominently displayed, whenever
they appear in public. Today, all over England, congregations and crowds gather to recall together the dead of
two World Wars and a host of smaller combats. Today,
the politicians assembled as usual before the cameras in the
line-up at the Cenotaph, there have been church parades
and marches of veterans, and the usual media coverage.

I have lived in England for forty-five years now, and I
still haven't got used to this particular bit of English culture and English identity. I was brought up in the
Republic of Ireland, in a nationalist family of which
several members, including my father, had fought on the
Republican side in the Irish War of Independence and the
Civil War that followed it: 1916, the year of the Somme,
was for us the year of the Easter Rising in Dublin, of the
proclamation of Independence, and the beginning of what
Yeats called the 'terrible beauty' of the struggle that led to

the foundation of the Irish Free State and, ultimately, the Republic. So the Sunday nearest 11 November simply did not feature in our calendar. To remember the dead is to accept kinship with them, and in the world where I grew up no one wanted to claim kinship with the dead of the two World Wars. My mother's father had been a British soldier, who had fought in both the Boer War and the First World War, and my grandmother, a former British army washerwoman, lived in a street of houses built for ex-servicemen and called Legion Avenue. Yet we took no pride in that dimension of our family's past, and felt little curiousity about it.

In all this, we were entirely typical. No one remembered, much less honoured, the tens of thousands of Southern Irishmen who fought and died for England in those conflicts; no one sold poppies in our streets; and the war memorials at the roadside or the centre of the country towns of my childhood commemorated other dead, in conflicts nearer home.

For it was a culture saturated with remembrance of war, and the dead of war. Only, it was a different war, and one in which England was not the beloved fatherland, but the hated enemy. Every child at school was steeped in the rhetoric of nationalism, a rhetoric in which the illustrious dead were absolutely central. I remember learning by heart the Panegyric pronounced by Padric Pearse at the grave of the Fenian veteran, O'Donovan Rossa, in August 1915, and I can recite passages of it still:

Life springs from death; and from the graves of patriot men and women spring living nations. [The British] think that they have pacified Ireland. They think that they have purchased half of us and intimidated the other half. They think that they have foreseen everything, think that they have provided against everything; but the fools, the fools, the fools! – they have left us our Fenian dead, and while Ireland holds these graves, Ireland unfree shall never be at peace.

The Fenian and Republican dead were our dead, and in recalling them we knew who we were. It was a profoundly tribal act of recollection, as most remembrances are, and there was no room in it for the dead of another and opposing tribe, even when those dead had come from among our own communities, our own families. Ten years ago today, you may recall, IRA bombers planted explosives in an empty building opposite the Enniskillen War Memorial on Remembrance Sunday, and detonated them during the service, an atrocity made memorable even in the long and appalling annals of Ulster violence by the Christian dignity and moral greatness of the response of Gordon Wilson, whose daughter Marie was killed in the blast. But the bombers could be confident that their explosion would kill no one of Republican convictions, for what they were bombing was another tribe's ritual, a British affair.

And the tribal character of what this nation is doing today is equally obvious. Remembrance Day is about far more than remembering the past, and the dead who made the past: it is a way of rehearsing and reaffirming the roots of the present.

For many of those involved in Remembrance Day today, the events of the war were events in their own lives, the war dead were living human beings with names and faces, not abstractions but real people, loved or loathed. For them, remembrance is a poignantly human act, often an acknowledgement of hurts which have never been healed. But for most of us, that isn't so. Why do so many people, who have no direct experience of war, wear poppies, value Remembrance Day? One of the most powerful reasons is surely because the dead armies of the past are conscripts in our present business of constructing an image not of who they were, but of who we are. For Mr Portillo, for example, the war dead demand that we don't sell out to the greasy foreigners of the European Union; for others, no doubt, they plead, just as eloquently, that we can't and mustn't stand aside from involvement in the moral community of Europe.

For the dead don't speak: they are dumb and passive in our remembrances, they are at our mercy, and if we choose to treat them so, they become ventriloquist's dummies through whom we utter the words we think we need to hear. There is a profound but unintended symbolism about the fact that the nation's memorial to the war dead should be the grave of an unknown soldier, whose anonymity can do nothing to confound with human particularity the abstractions and the ideals we load upon it. We remember the dead on our terms.

In a way, I suppose, that needn't matter. For over a thousand years Christian pilgrims have made their way through dangers and discomforts to the shrine of St James at Compostella: at that shrine, miracles have been done and lives transformed. And yet, I am told by a most distinguished and generally reliable member of my College that the shrine at Santiago de Compostella may well contain the bones, not of the Apostle James, but of Priscillian, a heretic executed for his opinions in 386. And you may recall the savage little poem of Thomas Hardy in *Satires of Circumstance*, where grieving women quarrel for possession of a grave where each has had a child buried, and from which, unknown to any of them, the children's bones have been removed to make way for a new drainage system: but, as the sexton remarks,

> . . . as well cry over a new-laid drain
> As anything else, to ease your pain.

But one of the oddest things about our commemoration of the war dead is the improbable process of canonization which takes place within it. This doesn't of course apply only to soldiers: two months ago we had an astonishing demonstration of the process of instant canonization, in the national idealization of Princess Diana.

Maybe we shouldn't be surprised by this. There is, of course, in death itself a sort of moral armistice, the annihilation of all difference within that fellowship of silence. Death is a single fate that makes all quits, and wipes out the distinction between German and English, enemy and ally, good and bad: 'I am the enemy you killed, my friend,' says the dead German in Wilfred Owen's *Strange Meeting*, 'let us sleep now.' But Owen's perception of the common humanity of suffering men and women caught up in the senselessness of war is almost the opposite of the idealizing of the war dead which seems to be an ineradicable part of the process of Remembrance. Fallible, frail, sinful human beings, some of them cowards, some of them liars, some of them adulterers or cheats, are transfigured by the simple fact of their death in uniform into secular saints, war heroes. Some of them were heroes, of course. But for many, their deaths were without much glory, swept along by the tide of events, conscripted into armies whose objectives they knew little about and in whose decision-making they had no share. They were not the heroes of war, but its victims, every bit as passive as the populations of the cities of Britain and Europe flattened under the rain of enemy bombs.

Once the idealizing of the war dead would have been given theological clothing. Padraic Pearse deliberately surrounded the Irish Rebellion with the language of blood sacrifice, redemption, Calvary: the Rebellion itself is invariably referred to in the Nationalist tradition as 'The Easter Rising', a phrase which, in a culture as saturated as that of Ireland with Christian thinking, sets off a formidable train of associations and interpretations. And, in much the same way and at the same time, during the First World War, English and German clergy scrambled over themselves to sprinkle holy water over the war effort and to canonize the fallen in all seriousness: the Bishop of

London, Winnington Ingram, didn't hestitate to claim that 'Christ died on Good Friday for Freedom, Honour and Chivalry, and our boys are dying for the same things'; 'Have no misgiving.'

Those who actually have to fight wars, of course, tend to have misgivings. Siegfrid Sassoon savagely pilloried clerical attempts to see the hand of God in war, or to marginalize the human suffering of the men in it by idealizing them:

> The Bishop tells us: 'When the boys come back
> They will not be the same; for they'll have fought
> In a just cause: they lead the last attack
> On Antichrist: their comrades' blood has bought
> New right to breed an honourable race,
> They have challenged death and dared him face to face.'

> 'We're none of us the same,' the boys reply
> 'For George lost both his legs; and Bill's stone blind
> Poor Jim's shot through the lungs and like to die
> And Bert's gone syphilitic: you'll not find
> A chap who's served that hasn't found *some* change.'
> And the Bishop said 'The ways of God are strange.'

But even the Second World War, so clearly a struggle against a profoundly evil and murderous tyranny, seems more ambivalent to us now: the defeat of Nazism was certainly something worth dying for, and even killing for; but the moral high ground the Allies could legitimately

claim seems less secure in the light of what we now know
about the bombing of Dresden, Hiroshima, Nagasaki, or
the multiple betrayals of the people of Eastern Europe and
the Balkans in the carving up of the continent which
followed the War.

But, by and large, we do not remember the dead to be
made uncomfortable, or to be reminded of our moral
ambivalences. T.S. Eliot might declare that 'the communication of the dead is tongued with fire', but Remembrance Day is about the consolidation, not the
questioning, of our sense of ourselves. Behind the attraction of the ceremonies of poppies and wreath-laying is a
nostalgia for a sense of shared value, a longing for moral
clarity. War unites nations, silences divisions, sharpens
choices. As we commemorate the ending of the Second
World War, we look back yearningly to a world in which
evil was plain, out there, and wearing an enemy uniform;
when we were one nation, united by adversity and a
common foe. The remembrance of war is a reassurance
that, however hazy our moral horizons, however confused
our sense of collective identity, in that struggle and that
shared past there is firm ground, a place to rest, a flag. The
remembrance of war affirms us, it is a security.

And almost always a security *against* others. The
remembrance of war might seem to provide a bridge to
the suffering of others: it is one of the tragedies of human
societies that it rarely does so. The reality is that most of
our collective remembrance is not a true remembering,
but a selective forgetting. For really to remember war, and
the dead of war, would be to confront the moral

ambiguity and the shared guilt which war always involves. War is never glorious, never a good, though it may sometimes be the lesser of evils. To remember war, for Christians, is to come face to face with the reality of sin, and the web of failure and compromise which surrounds even our best-intentioned collective action. War some-times involves victory over a measurable evil: the downfall of a tyranny, the opening of prison doors. But it always involves the failure of human communication, the exal-tation of hatred into a virtue, the calculated destruction of the innocent along with the guilty. There are no innocent combatants, and no victors. There is no true remembrance which is not also, and first of all, repentance.

For Christians, of course, every Sunday is Remem-brance Sunday, for at the heart of Christian worship and Christian identity is an act of remembrance, the recol-lection of a man whose death we speak of in terms of warfare and victory:

> Sing my tongue, the glorious battle
> Sing the ending of the fray
> Now about the Cross, the trophy,
> Sound the loud triumphal lay.

And yet the remembrance involved in the Eucharist sets a disturbing question mark against the Remembrance we keep today, against all our remembering; for it is designed not, as they are, to consolidate our identities and our assurances, but to trouble and unsettle them. 'Why have you come to disturb us?,' asks the Grand Inquisitor of the returning Christ in Dostoevsky's fable. In Christ, indeed, the communication of the dead *is* tongued with fire.

The very description of Christ's death as a victory presses the concept of victory to the limits of meaning, for what sort of a victory is it that involves the humiliation, torture and destruction of the victor, the scattering of his supporters, the disproof of his teaching? In the Eucharist we celebrate as a conqueror a man who is patently nothing of the sort, but a victim. In the commemoration of war we define ourselves as a people by recalling our conflicts with other peoples, our triumphs over a rival community. The God and Father of our Lord Jesus Christ calls us to be a people founded not on strength, not even on the triumph of right over wrong, but on weakness and solidarity with the weak, on the defeat of right by wrong. The victory of Christ is a victory unlike any other victory, because it involved the rejection of any type of force, and it was won at no one else's expense. Against our self-construction, against our hijacking of the dead and the past to justify our present, the Eucharist calls to a true remembrance, and against our rhetoric sets the silence of one who stood with the defeated, and descended among the dead.

As we make our remembrance today, as the princes and peers and politicians assemble, that silent figure is among us, in judgement, as he stood once in judgement before Pilate, who imagined himself to be the judge. In him there stand before us all the world's victims, all those at whose cost what we and every other nation count as victories are won: the children of Hiroshima, the dead of the battle-fields and the blitzed cities and the camps, the starving, whose necessities weigh less with us and our governments than the demands of the arms industry. The living Lord of the Eucharist is the ghost at our feast of Remembrance.

But he comes in forgiveness as well as judgement. Remembering war, we recall not just our culpability, but our predicament, the brokenness of a world in which wars occur and will go on occuring, a world in which our attempts at mending so often seem to end in violence, where even our good intentions somehow bring ourselves and other people to grief. Remembering him, we can lay hold on the mercy of a God who has taken into himself all our enmities, who has absorbed as victim the world's hatred and fear, who returns nothing for our violence but love, and who offers us, despite our wars, a share in his victory. We have only to lay down our arms, and to learn to struggle using only his.

4

The fish breakfast

Jesus College, Oxford, 1994
Readings: Jn 21

In our culture, to forgive is often to forget: we don't take sin very seriously, instead we preach self-acceptance. We are encouraged by psychotherapists, salesmen and even clergy to feel good about ourselves. A sense of guilt is, by general consent, an unhealthy thing. This is reflected in a lot of what passes for Christianity. The Good News is the news that God doesn't really mind our sins very much: they are easily forgiven, for they are not very serious. There is no hell, no judgement, no condemnation. God is nice, and in him there is no nastiness at all.

The twenty-first chapter of St John's Gospel is a story about the abundance of God's forgiveness, which nevertheless undermines these assumptions. It is a story of forgiveness, rehabilitation and new life: a story of resurrection. But it is a rehabilitation which begins in grieving and ends in crucifixion. If we want to learn the Christian meaning of forgiveness, this is a good place to begin.

The chapter itself is a sort of Chinese puzzle, which becomes more and more complicated the more you investigate it. For a start, it has clearly been tacked on to the completed Gospel, which comes to a decisive end with the previous chapter: 'Now Jesus did many other signs which are not written in this book, but these are written that you may believe that Jesus is the Christ, the Son of God, and that believing, you may have life in his name.'

And the extra chapter itself is a puzzle. It seems to tell one single story, about an encounter of the risen Christ with Peter and some of the other apostles in Galilee, but you can see quite clearly that two stories have been run together here: one about a miraculous draught of fishes, to which Peter responds with a threefold declaration of love, upon which he is appointed shepherd of Christ's sheep, and told he will follow his Master even to death on a cross; and a quite different story about the appearance of the risen Christ at a fish meal, which he shares with the apostles, who, as in so many of the resurrection stories, have difficulty recognising him. Both these stories have close parallels in St Luke's Gospel – the miraculous draught of fishes in Luke 5, and the fish meal after the Resurrection in Luke 24. The similarities and the differences between Luke's and John's versions of these stories are fascinating, but this is a sermon not a seminar, so I won't bother you with them now. But we do need to remind ourselves of the way Luke tells the story of the miraculous draught of fishes, in order to see how it has been turned almost upside down in John.

In Luke 5, Jesus puts to sea in Simon Peter's boat, and they go out into the deep. Peter has been fishing all night long and caught nothing, but at Jesus' command lets his nets out again, and catches so many fish that the nets begin to tear, and he has to summon his partners in another boat to help. Both ships are filled to sinking point with fish. The terrified Simon falls at Jesus' feet, and begs him to depart from him, because he is a sinful man. Jesus tells him and his companions not to be afraid: from now on they will be fishers of men. And coming to land, they leave everything, and follow him.

For Luke, this is a story of beginnings, the start of the apostles' journeyings with Jesus. It begins with men who are living an ordinary life in the world, but who leave that once and for all to become disciples. For John, however, this is a story which is the very reverse, for now the story comes not at the beginning of Jesus' ministry, but after it has ended; and we are dealing not with men who were once fishermen and are about to become apostles, but men who were once apostles and who have abandoned discipleship to become fishermen again. When Peter announces at the beginning of this story that 'I am going fishing' he is doing more than announcing how he intends to pass the evening. He is reneging on the irrevocable call which has made him a fisher of men, and he is leading his fellow disciples astray. This, as the writer will soon remind us, is the Peter who has already denied Jesus three times.

All commentators agree that, in its original form, this story embodies an ancient tradition, found also in St Matthew, that the first encounter of the apostles with the risen Christ happened not in Jerusalem, but in Galilee. That explains the odd scenario, the otherwise baffling fact that they are back in Galilee, fishing. Scattered by the crucifixion, they have returned to their old jobs, and have begun to forget the new life they had once lived with Jesus: they are once more simply partners in a fishing firm. In all the Gospels, the first resurrection experiences happen 'very early in the morning' – and so it is now. As they fish, unsuccessfully, in the dawn light, a dimly seen figure appears on the shoreline. They do not know him. Only when his instructions to cast their net on the right side of the boat result in an instantaneous bumper catch does anyone cotton on to his identity. Up to this point we have heard nothing about John, the beloved disciple – he's not in the list of apostles present at the beginning of the chapter – but he now suddenly appears to share this resurrection experience with Peter, as he had been with him at the empty tomb in the preceeding chapter: sensitized by love, he says 'It is the Lord.' But whereas in the empty tomb story this beloved disciple runs ahead of Peter and arrives first, now in his eagerness Peter leaps into the sea, pausing only to make himself decent, to greet the Lord.

And it is as if John has gone out of his way to draw a contrast with Luke's version of this story. In Luke, the disciples are out in the deep sea; John tells us they were near the land. In Luke, the fish are brought into the boats, and fill them to the gunwales; in John, they cannot get them inside the boat at all, and drag them to shore in the net. In Luke, the nets break; in John, we are told the single net was untorn. In Luke, Peter begs Christ to go away; in, John, he rushes to be with him.

Ever since Christians began commenting on this story, it has been realized that all these points of detail are loaded with significance, though there hasn't always been agreement about just what that significance might be. From St Jerome in the fourth century to Bultmann in the twentieth, for example, everyone is agreed that the meal with fish and bread is meant to remind us of the feeding of the five thousand, and so of the Eucharist. And that net, which holds a great multitude of fish but does not tear, by common consent stands for the Catholic Church, which now as then holds some very queer fish indeed, keeping in a God-given unity multitudes of people who by all normal criteria have nothing in common. In the same way, everybody agrees that the oddly precise number of fish − 153 − is not just vivid factual reportage (though of course, it may be that too) but must have a symbolic meaning. But nobody can agree about what that meaning is, precisely. St Jerome thought (mistakenly, as it happens) that ancient writers on natural history had said there were exactly 153 different species of fish, and so the number means every race upon the earth in the net of the church. St Augustine noticed that if you add all the numbers from 1 to 17 together − 1+2+3+4+5+6 and so on − the sum is 153, and the number 17 itself is made up of the sacred numbers 10 and 7; so the number in the text is mystical shorthand for sum total without remainder − completeness and fulfilment. Professor Emerton, the Regius Professor of Hebrew here in Cambridge, in a famous article written nearly forty years ago, argued that the number 153 is actually the numerical equivalent of the consonants in the Hebrew place names Engedai and Eneglaim, where, according to the prophet Ezekiel, in the days of the

Messiah fishermen will spread their nets while the river of life, teeming with fish, will water the land.

We need not bother ourselves too much about these interpretations. For what stays in the memory from this chapter is the unforgettable confrontation between Peter and Jesus. For centuries, this conversation has been hotly contested between Christians. It is a key passage for the Roman Catholic understanding of the Petrine office in the Church, seen not as something which died with Peter himself, but as a reality which remains a living element in the Church of every age. For Protestants, by contrast, this story has no such continuing relevance, or only a generalized one: the Interpreter's Bible Commentary, for example, ignores the distinction Christ seems to make here between Peter and the other apostles – 'Simon, son of John, do you love me *more than these*?' – and says categorically that the authority given to Peter here is given to him as a representative of all the apostles.

Whatever we may think about those issues of church and authority, it is in this face-to-face encounter between the Lord who was betrayed and the disciple who has betrayed him that we learn something of what the Resurrection means for us, what it means to be forgiven. In the previous chapter, the Risen Lord breathes the Spirit upon the apostles, and tells them that 'If you forgive the sins of any, they are forgiven: if you retain the sins of any, they are retained.' Peter stands before his Lord now to be forgiven, both as disciple and as betrayer.

In this Gospel, judgement is never an external thing, the vengeance of God imposed from above: we judge

ourselves, as Pilate judges himself, by our response to
Christ. The judge is not the frightening figure coming on
the clouds or seated on a throne, but the silent broken
man in the crown of thorns. And so it is here: the Lord
says nothing directly of the betrayal in the house of the
High Priest enacted beside a charcoal fire, as this meeting
is. Instead, he simply holds a mirror up to Peter. At the
Last Supper Jesus had told the disciples that where he was
going they could not follow, but that they would follow
later. Peter, well-meaning as always but totally self-
centred, and very sure of his own pre-eminence, blustered
in, 'Why can't *I* follow you, I who would lay down my
life for you.' In reply, Jesus predicts his fall: 'Lay down
your life for me? I say to you, before the cock crows, you
will deny me three times.'

In tonight's Gospel, Jesus offers him the same chance to
push himself forward. 'Simon, son of John, do you love
me more than these others do?' But Peter, who would
formerly have relished that question, and who has rushed
ashore to be the first to greet Jesus, for once is abashed. He
refuses to set his love in competition with the love of
others, and the ground of his confidence has moved from
himself, to Christ: 'Lord, *you know* that I love you.' And so
Christ replies, 'Feed my lambs.' Coming after the coolness
of the way in which Christ has addressed him, using his
formal patronymic – like saying 'Dr Timothy Jenkins',
instead of 'Tim' – this is a staggering act of trust: Peter
here is to take on the role of the Good Shepherd, the
identity of Christ himself. But in this moment of exalta-
tion his humbling is only beginning. As if he had not

heard the first time, Christ asks again, and then again, 'Simon son of John, do you love me?' Peter's reply to the third repetition, 'Lord, you know everything, you know that I love you,' is at one and the same time a confession of faith – the equivalent of Thomas' 'My Lord and my God' – and a cry of pain wrenched from him by the knowledge that his threefold betrayal has been rebuked by this threefold questioning of his love.

And now that terrible conversation at the Supper, when he had so arrogantly and ignorantly demanded the right to follow Christ and to lay down his life for him, is marvelously fulfilled. Once more entrusting his sheep to him, Christ tells him that, 'When you were young you girded yourself, and walked where you wanted: but when you are old, you will stretch out your hands and another will bind you and carry you where you do not wish to go.' The shepherd will lay down his life for Christ's sheep. Peter the betrayer, the runaway, will become the image of the Master he had three times denied, and will himself be led away to be crucified. No one is punished in John's Gospel, except Christ. It is not sin, but forgiveness, which brings suffering in its train.

Sin in St John's gospel is no light matter: it is a terrible thing, inevitably bringing judgement. But judgement is not suffering: it is its opposite, self-absorbed insensitivity. Peter's betrayal matters desperately. It has distanced him from Christ, it has led him back to the aimlessness of his old life, and it must be reversed. The arrogant self-assurance which betrayed him into his denials and the abandonment of discipleship must be undone, and its undoing will be full of grief. He must learn not to lord it over others, not to measure his love in competition. And this process of learning is lifelong, never-ending. It is part of the artistry of the Gospel writer, and of the greatness of John's theology, that even after being forgiven and confirmed as shepherd, Peter slips into just this sort of competitive curiousity about the discipleship and destiny of others: 'Lord, what about this man,' he asks, and is once again scathingly rebuked: 'What business is that of yours: just follow me.'

The Christ of this story is generous, the provider of living bread, the author of a salvation as abundant as all the fishes of the sea. But he is also stern, inflexible, questioning: not moved by easy declarations of love, unrelenting in pointing to the consequences of true discipleship in a world which stands under judgement for its – and for our – rejection of the Light which has come into the world, that Light which has shown us what it means, and what it costs, to be truly human.

5

Christianity and culture

Kings College, Cambridge, 2000
Readings: Wis. 7:15–30; 1 Cor. 2:1–8

I have been asked to speak tonight about the relationship of
the Gospel to the arts. It is an invitation I regretted
accepting almost as soon as I began to think what I might
actually say. In this building, after listening to this choir,
and looking eastward to the glory of Rubens' great painting
of the Adoration of the Magi, any sensible preacher must
feel that the only possible thing to do is to shut up, and let
the surroundings and the service speak for themselves: for
here is the relationship of Christianity to culture. In this
building, human ingenuity and human invention have
turned mountains of stone into acres of lace, and have filled
the gaps with a Bible in glass: the story of the redemption
and final destiny of the human race is set out here in walls
made of coloured light. And to add hearing to vision, day
by day the meaning of that story is elaborated and celebrated in great music, music which recapitulates the highest
achievements of European art for half a millennium.

And not only Europe: the psalms we heard sung are
Tudor prose poems, translations of Near Eastern texts

which were already immemorially ancient when Christ
was born. In their noble word-patterns are encoded most
of the fundamental human emotions: aspirations, weak-
enesses, war and peace, hope and fear, faith and doubt,
love and hate, rage and gentleness, birth and marriage and
death. If you are looking for a real Millennium Dome, not
a theme park but a place in which two thousand years of
Christianity are celebrated and made sense of in art, this is
as good a place to start as any. This chapel is a witness to
the conviction that in the beauty of holiness, beauty of
eye, ear, and mouth, as skillful and perfect as all the human
arts can make it, we can glimpse the heart of God.

And in fact, a huge proportion of the creative energy of
our culture has been poured into religion. From the fourth
to the nineteenth centuries, Christianity provided Europe
with its dominant ideology: its stories shaped our morality,
our family structures, our ideas about sovereignty and
society, the relations of rich and poor; and in all that the
arts played a crucial role, encoding, endorsing, expressing
and sometimes criticizing Christian civilization. The
National Gallery in London in the year 2000 ran an
exhibition to mark that Millennium. It was called *Seeing
Salvation*, and it explored the representation of Christ in
art through the centuries. It wasn't a large show, just a few
rooms of carefully chosen objects, but in his introduction
to the catalogue the Director of the Gallery pointed out
that more than a third of all the pictures in the National
Gallery are religious, and more than half of *them* portray
the face or life of Christ. Our whole culture has been
shaped by, and has helped to shape, our religion.

Despite this, Christianity has always had a problem about beauty, and eloquence, and skill. Christians have taken to heart the description of the Suffering Servant in Isaiah 53, which they have understood as a prophecy about Jesus:

> He hath no form and comeliness, and when we shall see him, there is no beauty that we should desire him. He is despised and rejected of men, a man of sorrows, and acquainted with grief, and we hid as it were our faces from him.

So there has been a persistent sense among Christians that beauty conceals God as much or more than it reveals him, that art does not always lead us beyond itself to God, but instead is likely to trap us with earthly beauty. There have always been Christians who thought that the arts had no place in religion, because they seduce the senses rather than elevate the mind; there have always been Christians who thought that the only paint permissable in Church was whitewash. St Augustine, for example, knew that moving and well-performed music was an asset in worship; but in a famous passage in his *Confessions* he describes his great uneasiness as a bishop when the music in church was *too* good, distracting him and the congregation from the message, with sheer pleasure in the medium itself: 'I have sometimes gone so far', he tells us, 'as to wish to banish all the melodies and sweet chants commonly used from David's psalter from my ears and from the Church as well.' In the same spirit, C.S. Lewis once claimed that

banal and ugly hymns were best, because then we concentrate on what they are saying, and not the way they say
it. Both of them would have been uneasy in this chapel.

There is more to all this than philistine puritanism:
behind this distrust, there is the fear that there is some sort
of mismatch between what human art can accomplish, and
what God is actually like. The more wonderful the art is,
the more likely we are to have the experience but to miss
the meaning: the art becomes the rival of the God it is
supposed to reveal. This is not as implausible as it may
sound. Consider the crowds who flock to this chapel to
listen to Evensong, day after day. Many, of course, are
believers, but many are not: they come to hear glorious
music in a glorious building, one of the greatest cultural
tourist stops in the world. We have no windows into
other people's souls, and no doubt for many this is an
experience which carries powerful news from heaven,
intimations of immortality and a challenge to the daily
routine of getting and spending. But for many others it is
like going to the opera or playing a CD, culture Classic
FM-style – art and religion, twin amenities of the civilised
life: relax, unwind, no need to feel challenged at all.

These conflicting perceptions of the value of human
culture as a vehicle for the Divine are reflected in tonight's
readings. The author of the Book of Wisdom puts what he
has to say in the mouth of Solomon, the king of ancient
Israel, who was believed to have been the fountain of
wisdom himself, master of all the arts and sciences, of all
human learning and skills. For Solomon, all these arts are
uncomplicatedly good, because they flow from God

himself, the Divine Wisdom who inspires and enables everything that is good and beautiful and true. Wisdom is the worker of all things, the pure and most subtle spirit which lights up the human mind and the human imagination. So art, all art and not just the religious kind, comes from God, and tells us something about him.

And that is the generous vision which inspires that marvellous picture by Rubens above the altar there, the Adoration of the Magi. For Rubens, the Magi represent what Solomon represented for the author of Wisdom: human learning, skill, imagination, the human mind and the human soul at full stretch, weary with travel in search of the ultimate beauty and truth, but pressing on in the conviction that ultimate beauty and truth can be grasped, indeed, will give themselves to the earnest seeker. And in the picture, that conviction is rewarded. Art brings us to the brink of faith, and faith to the edge of vision. The old king who kneels so eagerly to the Christ Child is thought by some to be a self-portrait of Rubens himself, his gesture of adoration and longing a metaphor for his art and the dedication of his life. And before him is what his art has brought him into contact with: a wonderfully warm and humane vision of the divine, personified in the glorious smiling womanhood of Mary, and the approachable tenderness of her child. There could be no sunnier portrayal of the conviction that art can serve faith and reveal God to us.

But the same scene can be portrayed in quite a different way. In the National Gallery exhibition, there was another picture of the Adoration of the Magi, this time by Breughel, and it tells a different story. In Breughel's picture, the Christ Child is encircled by the kings and their followers. Ugly men whisper and stare. Steel-helmeted soldiers, with brutal leering expressions, stand against the horizon, blocking the light, their spears and halberds a cruel forest of metal, making sinister sharp-edged crosses against the sky. The kings themselves are personifications, not of wisdom and skill, but of craft and cunning, their faces ravaged, their hair clinging to their scalps like unclean spiders' webs, their eyes hooded and blind or fierce and staring. In Breughel's picture, as in Rubens', an old man kneels to the child; but Breughel's ancient king offers a basin filled with myrhh, the spice used to embalm the dead. The terrified child recoils into the shelter of his mother's lap, but instead of consoling him she urges him to accept the myrrh, pointing with her hand to the coming horror. If Rubens' picture is an illustration of our reading from the Book of Wisdom, Breughel's is an illustration of the passage from Paul. The kings are the princes of this world, blind to the true nature of the child before them, their wisdom reduced to craftiness: they prefigure the rulers, Pilate and Caiaphas, who will crucify the Lord of glory.

Of course Breughel's picture, just as much as Rubens', is itself a triumph of art: we are not in fact dealing with a demonstration of the inadequacy of human skill or art or wisdom to say anything true of God, to recognise who Christ is, but an example of just how powerfully art can do precisely that. But the Breughel picture is informed, in a way that Rubens' Adoration is not, by a suspicion of human art and human achievement, and by the sense that when God comes into the world, human ingenuity and skill seek him out, not to adore, but to kill him.

For Breughel, as for Paul, worldly wisdom, skill, rule, the human arts and faculties embodied in the Magi and in the figure of Solomon, are dedicated not to life but to pain and destruction, and the arts are implicated along with the rest of human culture, a culture which in Breughel's violent age as in ours can be described in Pope John Paul II's words, as a culture of death. Unaided human attempts to make sense of the world construct patterns of destruction more often than of order and beauty. That is why there is a deep biblical tradition that the truth of God is uttered without art: in the Old Testament, Moses is a stammerer. Christians too have explored the idea that in becoming incarnate God makes himself dumb and artless – the Eternal Word of God, whose voice shaped the heavens and the earth, becomes a child with no voice except a cry: the Word within a word unable to speak a word. And Christ chooses his apostles not from the rhetoricians or wordsmiths, but from among uneducated fishermen whose broad Galilean brogue marked them out as peasants, as W. H. Auden wrote of them,

> Without arms or charm of culture,
> persons of no importance
> from an unimportant province,
> they did as the Spirit bid,
> went forth into a joyless world
> of swords and rhetoric, to bring it joy.

Swords and rhetoric: power and art. You can see that mixture here in this chapel: this is not just the house of God or a temple of culture, it is a place of kings. The carved roses and portcullises so beautifully lit in the ante-chapel were placed there to annex this building to the service of earthly power, the power of the Tudor dynasty, a power established, like most political power, on a foundation of blood. The artists who carved and painted and glazed here were serving God, no doubt; but also the princes of this world, who crucified the Lord of Glory. Artists are not inspired men and women with a hotline to the Sublime, to God. Art is not news from heaven, but a human construct, often deeply compromised, deeply implicated in networks of privilege, power, coercion. Rubens, that great and humane soul, was a court painter and a diplomat for the most powerful empire of his time.

And it has always been so: the very earliest symbolic representation of Christ in the National Gallery's *Seeing Salvation* exhibition was the Chi-Ro monogram, encoding the opening letters of the name 'Christ' in Greek. The monogram is on the reverse of a coin of the emperor Constantine struck in 327, fourteen years after he seized control of the Roman Empire by force. On his coin the name of Christ surmounts a war-banner, with the inscription 'The hope of the State': from the very beginning, Christian art was hijacked to serve the powerful and the successful.

There is no avoiding it: art is, after all, in the end, a form of heightened speech, one of the modes by which the human heart reveals itself to itself. We will find in art, even and perhaps especially religious art, only what is already in the heart of man. That means that art can indeed show us the image of God, for we ourselves have been created in that image. Looking at the Rubens, looking at the glory of the carved stones above our heads, we need not doubt that. But we need to remind ourselves that the child in Rubens' picture came to set a question mark against our notions of order, power, success; that he identified himself with, and mainly preached to, those outside the scope of art – the dumb, the downtrodden, and the poor; and that, when he came at last into the courts of priests and rulers, it was to be mocked and murdered. The real news from heaven comes to us each day in our newspapers, on our TV screens, as we hear of the sufferings of the world he came to save. The silent child beckons us away from the eloquence and the splendour, to see and serve him in his poor.

6

On not quite starting again:
Shrove Tuesday

Queen's College, Birmingham, 1987
Readings: Joel 2:12–18; 2 Cor. 5:20–6:2

Tomorrow Lent begins. For most of us, it is notionally an opportunity for renewal, a call to cleansing and rebirth; but actually, in my experience and probably in yours, a time of somewhat tepid resolve, when we embark on a regime of mild penitential observance – giving up coffee or getting up earlier, the substitution of something edifying for our bedside reading in place of the frivolities of P.G. Wodehouse or the snobbery with violence of Agatha Christie or Dorothy Sayers. It's an annual nod, in fact, in the direction of spiritual hygiene, designed, within reason, to toughen us up, and to eliminate some of the supernatural flab that most of us know we carry. Not all that different, in fact, from the regime of cold baths and stiff upper lip that was once felt to go to the making of an English gentleman, and with about the same degree of existential urgency.

And even in the ages of the Church in which Lent was taken more seriously, it had something dogged, stolid, stoical, about it; the ancient Lenten collects of the Roman Missal sound a matter-of-fact note again and again:

> Look favourably on the devotion of your people, Lord we pray, that as by abstinence our bodies are restrained, so by the fruit of good works our minds may be renewed [Thursday, Lent I]

The hope of renewal is there all right, but without much in the way of excitement or, for that matter, the sense of urgency and threat that saturates the reading we heard from Joel, and which has from time immemorial been used in the liturgy for the beginning of Lent. If you try to spell out the idea of the Christian life implicit in such prayers, you can't altogether avoid the feeling that the model being offered is that of a long slow pedal uphill, without much sense of whether or not the view is going to be worth it at the top. And looking back on my own religious formation, as a boy in pre-Vatican II Ireland, I have an impression that a lot of it was like that; it could be a grim religion, with effort at a premium, and a general sense that if you were going to get anywhere religiously, it was going to involve a fair amount of slog and unpleasantness. The discipline involved in such a religion was called 'mortification', deadening – and that often seemed a depressingly appropriate notion.

Certainly, it's not an easy notion for twentieth-century Christians to appropriate. By and large, we absorb our ideas of spiritual health from the assumptions of our culture; and to post-Freudian men and women there is something suspect about the idea of restraint, self-punishment, penitential self-absorption. Lent seems to epitomize self-hatred and self-control, when what we long for, and what we believe in, is self-realization. Most of us accept the twentieth-century heresy that holiness is wholeness, and by and large we think that the first step to loving God is to learn to love ourselves. Hence the contemporary Church's half-heartedness about the traditional penitential disciplines, symbolized in the Catholic Church's abolition of fasting, and its replacement with the genteel suggestion that it might be nice to do something ennobling on Fridays.

And in any case, the Lenten readings which we have heard are filled with an urgency which seems worlds away from the stolidity of Lent as most of us experience it. In Joel's trumpet call to repentance we are being beckoned to some strange renewal which brushes aside mundane concerns, that wrenches us out of normality – call a solemn assembly, gather the people, let the bridegroom leave his room, and the bride her chamber. And Paul is every bit as urgent – we beseech you on behalf of Christ, be reconciled with God, now is the acceptable time, now is the day of salvation.

These are daunting passages; but they have a fascinating note of decisiveness and finality about them, an invitation to break with the past and to launch out into some new world of the spirit. There is a glamour about them, a sense of crisis, that matches something in modern Christian sensibility. So many of our saints and heroes are people like Dietrich Bonhoeffer or Simone Weil – loners,

pioneers, people whose faith has taken them away from
the comfortable and familiar, away from the world of slow
painful progress, men and women, in Kierkegaard's
phrase, 'out alone over ten thousand fathoms of water'.
That's more what we want to think of when we think of
Christian renewal – a call to begin all over again, to stride
outside and away from the sphere of the humdrum. And
part of its attraction has nothing to do with religion. It's
more the sense we all have at times of the need to break
away, to cut the chains of habit and surpass and maybe
surprise ourselves. That feeling has given rise to a lot of the
best opening lines in modern poetry – W.H. Auden's

> To throw away the key and walk away

or Lowell's

> O to break loose, like the Chinook
> Salmon jumping and falling back,
> Nosing up to the impossible
> Stone and bone crushing waterfall
> Raw-jawed, weak fleshed there, stepped by ten
> Steps of the roaring ladder, and then
> To clear the top on the last try,
> Alive enough to spawn and die.

or Philip Larkin's

> Sometimes you hear, fifth hand,
> As epitaph

He chucked up everything
And just cleared off.
And always the voice will sound
Certain you approve
This audacious, purifying
Elemental move.

But there's the rub: there is so little that is audacious, purifying, or elemental about our spiritual experience; so often it seems cyclical, not linear, an endless return to where we were before. And if anything, the annual routine of Lent emphasizes that disheartening repetitiveness, as our all-too-familiar, not quite fresh, beginnings reveal to us not new spiritual freedoms, but the extent to which we are the prisoners of our own reluctances, the depth of our unwillingness to be disturbed. The Pauline insistence that now is the day of salvation, that we must turn away from ourselves today, lest we receive the grace of Christ in vain, is so easily turned aside. One of the best of all modern religious poems, by Geoffrey Hill, catches this exactly:

What is there in my heart that you should sue
so fiercely for its love? What kind of care
brings you as though a stranger to my door
through the long night and in the icy dew

seeking the heart that will not harbour you,
that keeps itself religiously secure?
At this dark solstice filled with frost and fire
your passion's ancient wounds must bleed anew.

So many nights the angel of my house
has fed such urgent comfort through a dream,
whispered 'Your lord is coming, he is close'

that I have drowsed half-faithful for a time
bathed in pure tones of promise and remorse;
'Tomorrow I shall wake to welcome him'.

What Hill is charting there is our lack of will, maybe our
lack of freedom, to respond decisively. We have a fatal
tendency to turn even the prophetic or angelic call to go
out to meet the Lord into a piece of furniture, or one
more stone in the imprisoning wall of our securities, an
opportunity to 'bathe in pure tones of promise and
remorse'. We turn religion into a habit or a comfort,
instead of allowing it to be what the enigmatic and
questioning figure of the Gospels surely intended: a
question mark against our values and securities. And that is
one of the living paradoxes of Lent: at one and the same
time a challenge to our habit-bound existence, and itself a
clear example of it. Its call to self-denial ought to move us
one step nearer to leaving all and following the Christ
whose summons beckons us away from our earth-bound
existence. But in fact the piffling self-denials involved
seem more plausible as attempts to purchase the legitimacy
of those concerns in return for a token down-payment of
spiritual action – literally buying on the never-never system. There has always been in Christianity a tension
between the apparent timidities of such deliberate piety
and the aspiration for freedom in the spirit, for a

breakthrough into a new order. In the Lives of the Desert Fathers it is told how Abbot Lot came to Abbot Joseph and said,

> 'Father, I keep my little rule to the utmost, my fasts, meditation and contemplative silence; as much as I can I have striven to cleanse my heart. And now what?' And Father Joseph for answer stood up and stretched his hands to heaven, and his fingers were ten torches of fire. And he said, 'Why not be changed totally into fire.'

That's what we would like, to be changed totally into fire, and Abbot Lot's little rules, his Lent, seems the wrong way to go about it; like an unsuccessful boy scout rubbing away with two damp pieces of stick. Maybe something of this feeling underlay at least part of the Reformation debate about justification by faith. But I think all the same it's a wrong perception; for what the repeated infidelities of Lent, and of the Christian life, bring home to us, as maybe nothing else can, is precisely the precariousness and rarity of human freedom. The grand gesture is never effortless, and behind the miraculous balance and sanity of the great saints, behind their freedom, lies a relentless struggle against self. For Christian freedom, the freedom to be changed totally into fire, meets headlong our rootedness in earthy things. Christ calls us to follow him, but his road takes him outside the earthly city, outside the world of buying and selling, of marrying and giving in marriage, where most of us don't want to go, and can't go. And to

put it at its lowest, the unsuccessful disciplines of Lent
bring home to us the extent of our unfreedom, the depth
of our rootedness in and dependence on these things. To
discover the freedom of our true selves, to escape the
prison of our own assertive separateness, is not within our
power. We need to be rescued from our domestic uni-
verses, pitched headlong into awareness of our own
incompleteness, our need of one another and of God. It is
the traditional role of Christian discipline, of asceticism, of
Lent, to loosen our grip on the securities of everyday
living, even everyday Christian living, by testing the
extent to which we have become trapped by them. It's not
that the Church has ever believed that such disciplines
could simply grow into the freedom of the spirit; but it has
recognized in the challenge of hunger, or lack of sleep, or
abstinence from sex, a corrective to our tendency to forget
that we can barricade the spirit of God out, even with his
own good gifts.

Before Lent comes Carnival, before Ash Wednesday,
Shrove Tuesday: in the traditional Christian calendar there
is a recognition of dialectic, even of paradox. Lent is not,
therefore, a statement that the Christian way is life-
denying, built on a series of 'thou shalt nots'. But it is an
assertion that the soul which cannot say no even to the
legitimate good things of this world will never be free. We
must move, as the Gospel moves, not with balance and
moderation, but between affirmation and denial. The
Christian asceticism represented in Lent doesn't represent
a morbid fear of life and its good things, but a profound
wisdom in the tradition, which recognizes that it is

precisely the *good* things of God which can most successfully mask from us the terrible and wonderful reality of the Creator, and of ourselves. Not that things, the beauty of the world, food, art, money, sex, are bad; their power to tame us, to trap us, to make us settle down when it is our business to be travellers, comes precisely from their goodness. Yet they are *things*; if we rest in them we lose ourselves, and worse, we lose their Lord. And it is part of the tragedy of being human that we cannot love things and leave them. Dr Johnson, the greatest and wisest of all the saints of Anglicanism, was once taxed in old age by a Scotch hostess on his total refusal of alcohol. Surely a little wine from time to time was harmless and pleasant; moderation was surely a virtue? 'Madam', said Johnson, 'I *cannot* be moderate.' Christian discipline, the quest for mastery of the self, is aimed not at cool detachment, nor at moderation, but at the freedom to walk away from the good that is not God. Its characteristic form is not therapy, or exercise, but amputation. That is the meaning of Jesus' warning against riches, and the story of the rich young man who went sorrowing away.

There is an ancient Roman prayer which begs God's mercy and guidance that we may so pass through 'the good things of this world that we finally lose not the things that are eternal'. 'Transeamus per bona temporalia' – passing through the good things of time. Once again, the Gospel paradox: the things are good, but must be abandoned. Translators can never stomach it. Cranmer, when he turned that prayer into the wonderful collect for the fourth Sunday after Trinity in the Book of Common

Prayer silently dropped the word 'good'; the revisers of the modern Roman Catholic liturgy, Pelagian to a man, dropped the 'passing through' and turned the whole thing into a prayer for the good use of a good world. But the meaning and aim of Christian discipline, of Lent, is contained precisely in the paradox: we are not to deny the world, not to hate ourselves. But neither are we to settle down: we are simply to be free. And since we are men and not angels, that is a process both painful and beyond our power. It is the gift of the spirit, of Abbot Joseph's fire. And like all his gifts, it can never be presumed upon. It must be yearned for, laboured at, sought with tears, prayed down. We must live our Lent, waiting forty days in the upper room, or in the wilderness, until the fire falls, and we are made new.

All this is to say that Lent invites us to explore the paradoxes of a Gospel that both affirms our human needs, and beckons us to a way of discipleship that takes us beyond them. It does more though: it invites us to grasp that it is indeed a Gospel. There is, certainly, no escaping the uncompromising urgency of the scriptural calls to repentance and to endeavour which we heard earlier. The call to be reconciled to God involves the demand that we follow Jesus, and what is demanded is an enormous effort, a lifetime of effort, everlastingly inadequate, everlastingly to be begun over again. But it is also something more, and something better. In some sense which we cannot adequately grasp, but which every Christian comes to recognize with joy and gratitude, before and beyond all effort it is an invitation to share in a work already accomplished (and complete). Our faltering and failing discipleship is already achieved on that terrible but triumphant journey outside the city of our mediocrity, to Calvary.

'We too were represented there', says Augustine. 'What hung upon the cross, if it was not that humanity that He had taken from us? Christ nailed our weakness to the cross where, as the Apostle says, our old self was crucified with him.'

And that is why in the end all Christian discipleship, all following of Jesus, finds its meaning and its method not in our solitary struggle with ourselves, but in the Church, in the Eucharistic community, the community of those who give thanks. Joel's call to penitence is a call to stand with the priests between vestibule and altar, to sanctify the congregation. In that congregation we are indeed constantly recalled to the full demand of God, constantly confronted with the need of our neighbour, constantly reminded of our failures in the life of discipleship. But we are also given a share in the one true discipleship, Christ's own obedience, our failures compensated for and redeemed by the less half-hearted commitment of our brothers and sisters, as we bear one another's burdens. Above all, our littleness, our timidity in following, our need for the homely, the comfortable, and the familiar, our longing to stay amid the things that will not stay, all this is redeemed and consecrated. On God's table Sunday by Sunday we lay all that we are, our work and our woes, our best aspirations and our worst failures, all that God has given us, and all that we have made of it, good or ill. And in the mercy of God, all that is given back to us, purified and transformed by the fire of his Spirit, a coal from the altar to cleanse unclean hearts and lips, bread for the toilsome journey that will take us home.

7

The man in the crowd: Palm Sunday

Readings: Isa 50:4–7; Ps. 21; Phil. 2:6–11; Mk 14:1–15, 47

Today we begin the observance of Holy Week, the heart of the Church's year and the most solemn and memorable part of the Church's liturgy. Today all over the world congregations will re-enact Christ's entry into Jerusalem and will listen to the story of his trial and death; and as the week goes on we will recall the Last Supper and the washing of the disciples' feet, we will read the Passion on Good Friday and venerate Christ's cross, and finally on Holy Saturday night we will use light and darkness, fire and water to proclaim the mystery of Christ's Resurrection from the dead, and the new life that flows from him to all of us.

All of us have a place in these awe-inspiring cere- monies, but probably most of us feel that our place in them is anonymous, as one of the crowd. In this week we celebrate the redemption of the world, the drama of Jesus' living and dying for all of us. The events are almost too big to think about: since the beginning of the world, God has been searching for human beings cut off from Him by sin.

In the events we celebrate this week, that age-old estrangement between us and the God who made us and loves us was once and for all brought to an end. The story is a majestic one, remote and terrible, and as we stand in our places today, listening to the long account of Christ's passion, we may wonder where *we* fit in.

Of course, at one level every Catholic does know that we fit in: every parish priest in the country will see faces on Good Friday he never sees at any other time of the year. Ordinary men and women all over the world today will join in shouting 'Hail King of the Jews', or 'Crucify him', or 'He saved others, he cannot save himself'; but that very fact underlines the sense many of us have of the difficulty of relating our own individual ordinary lives to this great story of the salvation of the world, which happened so long ago, so far away. We stand by as it all sweeps past, one of the crowd.

If we listen carefully to St Mark's account of the Passion, though, which is the one read today, we may find help with this problem in an unexpected way. At one level, Mark's is the least human of the Gospel accounts of the death of Jesus. The story is told very baldly, without much explanation: we hear how Judas decides to betray Jesus, but Mark, unlike St John, is not the slightest bit interested in why Judas should have turned on his Lord like this. In Mark there is no need to look for any human explanations, because everything is going according to God's plan. Everything is to happen 'as the Scriptures say it will', and though Jesus suffers and is afraid in this story, he is nevertheless always in charge of events, always one jump ahead. He knows exactly where they are to eat the Passover, he knows who will betray him, he knows exactly when Peter will deny him. Mark never lets us forget that all this is happening to accomplish the prophecies, and he never lets us forget exactly who Jesus is. At the very beginning of his Gospel he had announced it – 'The beginning of the Gospel of Jesus Christ, the Son of God.' Now, at the end, the centurion will remind us: 'In truth this man was the Son of God.' Mark knows this, and wants us to know it. All is as God wants it, everything is according to plan.

It's all a bit impersonal, and quite unlike the mess and muddle of our lives. When we come to suffer, maybe in a bad marriage, or to die, in a car crash or a hospital bed with tubes sticking out of us, we are unlikely to feel serenely in control, we won't think that all is as it is meant to be. So what has it all to do with us?

There is one figure almost on the margins of today's Gospel who wanders into Jesus' story and then out again, almost without being noticed. It is Simon of Cyrene. Simon was a stranger, an African Jew 'up from the country', probably in Jerusalem for the Passover celebrations. As the military procession with Jesus stumbling under the weight of the cross passed him by, the soldiers seized Simon, maybe because he was obviously a stranger, maybe because he was a big man, and they made him carry the cross. Both Matthew and Luke mention the incident, but Mark, usually so abrupt and uninformative, adds a little human detail that we learn about from no one else. Simon, Mark tells us, was 'the father of Alexander and Rufus'.

We have no idea who Alexander and Rufus were, but obviously Mark expected the people for whom he wrote his Gospel to recognize them at once. Simon is identified because he is the father of two men they all knew. There can only be one explanation for this: Alexander and Rufus were Christians. Think about that. Simon was an ordinary man, no apostle, no saint, a man in the crowd like us. A foreign tourist minding his own business is dragged against his will into a public execution – and his life was changed. We know nothing more about him, except that his sons were Christians, so almost certainly he was a Christian too. With those few words – 'the father of Alexander and Rufus' – Mark lets us realize that this majestic pageant in which God's will is inexorably worked out is not an inhuman, pre-planned thing. It is an event for each and every one of us. In the midst of our own often very inconsequential lives, the man on his way to die on Calvary can reach out and touch us, change us, real people with real names, with kids and jobs and concerns of our own. Even a casual and unwilling encounter with Jesus, as he goes the way God has chosen for him, can make a difference.

We know nothing about the journey that brought Simon's children to Christian baptism. Did Jesus speak to him that day and thank him, or turn and look? Or was it just that the events of that Friday niggled and puzzled Simon, set him asking questions, talking to the disciples, listening to the Scriptures? As he returned to his interrupted journey, 'up from the country', did he begin to wonder about the man whose gallows he had carried, whose crueller journey towards death he had briefly shared? We can never know, only that what began that Friday morning brought Simon and his family to faith in the man they hanged that day.

As we stand in the crowd this week, we need to make Simon's journey *our* journey. The story we tell today, and will tell again and again this week, took place not for some great abstraction, the salvation of the world, but so that ordinary men and women, people like you and me, might have lives that have purpose and shape. Jesus passes us by in the crowd; but for each one of us he will turn and look, he will offer us a chance to share in carrying his cross, so that we in turn may pass on to our children or our neighbours a hope that life and death, even violent messy death in the sun outside Jerusalem, is not the end of everything.

Whoever we are, whatever the aims we set ourselves on our own journey, somewhere along the way Jesus waits for us, with a burden too heavy for him to carry. We may have trouble recognising him, but his cross will be plain enough – wherever there is poverty or sickness or loneliness, he waits for our helping hand. And if we reach out a hand to help, we will find it is Jesus who grasps it, as he grasped Simon, and held him, and his children, for his own.

8

Walking to Emmaus: Easter Day

Westminster Abbey, 1990
Luke 24: 13–35

Every Easter Sunday afternoon throughout my childhood I went for a walk, two miles out of the small Irish town in which I had been born, to the local cemetery. Like hundreds of other people I was following a dozen grey-haired men carrying rifles, marching to a brass band behind drums and banners. Often they were led by my father, as officer-in-charge of the flag party. At the graveyard the procession made its way to the Republican plot, with its granite monument to those who had fallen in the fight for Irish Freedom. There, those veterans of the Irish War of Independence and the Irish Civil War raised their rifles and fired a volley of shots over the grave, and the Last Post was played by a trumpeter. Everyone then went to say a prayer beside their own family graves, which had been spruced up in Holy Week especially for the occasion, and we all went home.

Those Easter afternoon walks to the graveyard have stayed with me, forty years on, for they were walks into meaning. That culture was profoundly Christian. But it was also profoundly nationalist. We were steeped in the story of how, at Easter 1916, a group of badly-armed heroes had summoned Irish men and women to the Republican tricolour, and had launched the Rebellion which had led, at last, to the founding of the modern Irish State. They paid for their gesture with their lives, and we thought of them not merely as heroes, but as martyrs. Our faith and our patriotism fused into a single whole: indeed, it was not always very easy to see where one stopped and the other began. The rebellion itself was universally referred to, complete with capital letters, as 'The Easter Rising'.

That sort of language sounds blasphemous now, but in the enclosed world of 1950s Irish nationalism, it brought with it a great sense of security, of fitness. It made sense of the political and historical experience of the people, just as our religious faith made sense of our individual lives. We were indeed an Easter people. There was struggle, suffering and death: yet there was also renewal, redemption, *Rising*. The world made sense. It conformed to primal patterns of renewal, as tangible as the spring in the hedgerows we had walked past on our march out of the town, or the flowers we laid on our family graves before we went back home to tea. And so that Easter afternoon walk, towards our dead, really did seem a walk into meaning. Death itself took on a power to shape us into a people, a power signalled by the flowers and rifle fire, the flags and trumpets.

And to enter this great church this Easter Sunday afternoon is also to walk among the dead, and into meaning. This is a house of graves, and what you see all around you was built by King Henry III in the thirteenth century over the grave of a holy king, Edward the Confessor. Henry built it because the bones of the royal saint seemed able to give force and meaning to the acts of his living successors: they were part of the divinity with which the living ruler was hedged about. And here, ever since, at the shrine of the dead king, the living kings and queens have come to be crowned and empowered.

What helped give meaning to the monarchy, gave meaning to every aspect of the life of the nation. Here was a serious house, in which the pattern that lay beneath all the accidents and ills of the world might be glimpsed. Here even death took on a shape, and burial here bestowed a sense of order, and importance. And so all around the grave of Edward were ranged the graves of other powerful men and women, above all the kings and queens of England, clustered in a circle of meaning around the shrine. And over the centuries they have brought here the bones, the ashes, or just the names of our significant dead, so that the tribe might see and know who and what it is. The power of this place to shape chaos, to bring meaning out of horror and death, was witnessed to after the First World War, when the corpse of an unknown soldier was brought here from the battlefields of Flanders, and buried before the West Door. It is now the most important grave in the church, a new shrine for people who no longer believe in saints like King Edward, yet still people who need to make sense of war and famine, death and suffering, just as much as any of our ancestors. Here too, we are invited to walk toward the dead, and into meaning.

But all that can involve terrible self delusion. The dead are passive, and can be manipulated; the meanings we find in them are often the meanings we bring with us. King Henry, building the security of the Plantagenet dynasty on the bones of a Saxon saint; or an establishment honouring its poets and artists only when they are safely dead; or a nation rallying its citizens round war graves, may not be finding meaning, but inventing it. In our own times, we can see all too clearly how opposing sides in Bosnia or Northern Ireland have recruited the dead into armies of hatred, for the destruction of the living. That walk into meaning can all too often deliver us into the power of death.

And in any case, even Christians nowadays find it harder and harder to believe that such a walk has a journey's end. Death seems all around us, meaningless, violent, random: a planeful of diplomats on an economic mission; a classful of primary school children in a peaceful Scottish town; an entire nation wiped out in Rwanda or Bosnia. The Resurrection is hard to believe in. It seems to belong to the world of fairy tale — angels in shining garments, empty tombs, miraculous appearances. But for us there are no messengers from heaven to tell us all is well, that the Lord is risen.

The Gospel story we heard read today as the second lesson describes our situation, for it describes an Easter Sunday walk into despair, which ends, against all expectation, with the discovery of faith, and hope and love. Though for many people it is the most moving and vivid of all the Resurrection stories, there is no magic here, no angels, no flags or trumpets. And there are no heroes, not even an apostle. Instead, there are just two people like ourselves, bewildered and rootless as we often are, their faith faltering and gone. This is a story about loss of direction and doubt turned to strong and joyful faith, but it is not done by spectacular demonstration. The methods Jesus uses to evoke faith in the story are the methods he uses now. The men on the road to Emmaus are ourselves.

The two disciples are on a journey away from Jerusalem: away from the Holy City, the place of revelation, and the scene of the saving events of Good Friday and Easter. They have turned their back on significant places, on meaning itself. Perhaps they were leaving the Church, on their way back to a life in which there was no great hope, no promise of a Messiah for the nation, or of meaning for themselves, but in which at least there would be no terrible disappointments, none of the desolation of Good Friday. Like us, they are voyagers, unsure of their bearings, and night is drawing on. And when they encounter a stranger on their journey they don't recognise Jesus: their eyes are held from seeing him, and they even get irritated at the stupidity of his questions to them: when he speaks they stand still, locked in their own hopelessness.

This is the turning point of the story, for Jesus begins to teach them, not with new revelations, but by opening up to them their own past. He leads them through the whole of the Jewish Scriptures, to show how his life and suffering and death really do make sense, that if only they could see it properly, this was the fulfillment they and all God's

people had been waiting for. And if their eyes are blinded,
yet his words reach their hearts. When they arrive at the
house where they are to spend the night, they hold on to
him: 'Stay with us, for it is nearly evening.' They sit down
to a meal. And now he does what he has done dozens of
times with them before. Taking bread he blesses it and
breaks it; and as he does so, their eyes are opened, and they
recognize him, and he vanishes from sight.

This is a warmly human story, but we are not meant to
think that it was the familiarity of friendship which tells
them who he is. The blessing and breaking of bread is not
here the start of *any* meal. It is the Eucharist; and they
recognize him not because of a familiar mannerism, but
because he has opened their eyes by explaining the
Scriptures to them. If this were just a story about an
appearance, you'd expect them to bewail his departure,
but they do no such thing. They are full of excitement and
faith, as they remember his teaching, and as life and hope
and meaning come flooding in on their despondency.
'Did not our hearts burn within us while he talked to us
on the road, while he opened to us the Scriptures?' And
now they know where they are, and more important,
where they ought to be: they hurry back to Jerusalem, to
meet with the rest of the disciples and to spread the news
that the Lord is risen.

Nobody knows where the biblical village of Emmaus is,
and that is as it should be, because its importance doesn't
come from its being a place seven miles outside Jerusalem:
in fact it is everywhere. The Lord who comes to these
bewildered disciples on their journey away from hope

comes in the same way *now*, to all of us, as we make our
journeys through life. Like the men on the road to
Emmaus, often we don't recognize him. But now, as then,
we can share together in the life of his body, in the
breaking of bread. Sunday by Sunday, he invites us to take
a walk into meaning, not to a place of tombs, not to seek
the living among the dead, but to hear again his words, to
walk with him on his way. There, however uncertain we
are, however weak our faith or faltering our hope, we find
food for the journey and companionship along the way.
There our hearts can respond to his word, to the promises
of the kingdom which he will bring, and which we can
work for. We will see no angels, there will be no flags or
trumpets, but we have no need of them. The Lord is near,
he is in the midst of us, he is known to us in the breaking
of the bread.

Stay with us Lord, for it is nearly evening. Be our
companion on the road: kindle our hearts and stir up
our hope, so that in the Scriptures and in the
breaking of bread we may learn to know you, the
redeemer of Israel, the redeemer of the world. Amen.

9

A Sermon for Ascension

Monastic Vespers, Magdalene College,
Cambridge, 1995
Luke 24 vs 50–3

We are coming to the end of Easter: this week we will
celebrate the final resurrection appearance, the Ascension;
ten days beyond that, the gift of the Holy Spirit at Pen-
tecost, the self-giving of God to remake human community and put an end to human alienation.

The feasts of Easter don't, of course, celebrate a series of
different events. They are in fact a series of explorations of
the meaning of one event: the death and rising of Jesus
Christ. They spell out for us what it means to believe the
Resurrection.

The New Testament tells the Ascension story in conflicting ways. In the Synoptic Gospels, and especially in
the writings of St Luke, the Ascension brings to an end an
extraordinary forty-day honeymoon, a period of special
intimacy, in which the risen Christ showed himself
repeatedly to the disciples: eating with them, teaching,
correcting. But in St John, Resurrection, Ascension and
the gift of the Holy Spirit all happen on Easter Day: in
John there is no decisive departure to put an end to the

post-Resurrection appearances – the Evangelist simply stops telling us about them.

But it is the Synoptic picture of a decisive departure that has really caught the Christian imagination: medieval artists liked to portray it almost comically, with Christ's feet disappearing into a cloud while the open-mouthed apostles gaze upwards to catch the last possible glimpse of the Lord they know they will see no more in this world.

That sense of the parting of the ways, the bereavement of Church and world as their Lord leaves them behind, has a power all its own. One of my colleagues in the Divinity Faculty harnessed it by writing a book with the title *Taking leave of God*, and the notion of such a leave-taking evoked from Newman one of the most characteristically Victorian passages in the *Parochial and Plain Sermons*:

Had He not had enough of earth? What should detain Him here, instead of returning to the Father, and taking possession of His throne? He delayed in order to comfort and instruct those who had forsaken Him in the hour of trial. A time had passed when their faith had all but failed, even while they had His pattern before their eyes: and a time, or rather a long period, was in prospect, when heavier trials far were to come upon them, yet He was to be withdrawn. They hitherto understood not that suffering is the path to glory, and that none sit down upon Christ's throne, who do not first overcome as He overcame. He stayed to impress upon them the lesson, lest they should still misunderstand the Gospel, and fail a second time. And having taught them fully, after forty days, at length He rose above the troubles of this world. He rose above the atmospheres of sin, sorrow and remorse, which broods over it. He entered into the region of peace and joy, into the pure light, the dwelling-place of angels, the courts of the Most High, through which resound continually the chants of blessed spirits and the praises of the seraphim. There He entered, leaving His brethren in due season, to come after him ... Yet, though forty days was a long season for Him to stay, it was but a short while for the apostles to have Him among them. What feelings must have been theirs, when He parted from them? So late found, so early lost again. Hardly recognized, and then snatched away.

That, I think, gets it exactly wrong. For what the New Testament makes clear again and again is that the Ascension of Christ is about his coming closer to us, not about his taking leave of us. We are not to stand gazing up to heaven, but to grasp that now God is unimaginably closer to us than ever before. In St John's Gospel, Christ rebukes Mary Magdalene – *noli me tangere* – precisely for clinging mistakenly to his material presence and thereby missing the nature of his true closeness to us. It is to your advantage that I go, he tells the apostles. What sort of leave-taking is no form of departure? Just what is it we will celebrate this week?

For Newman, the effect of the Ascension is that Christ is no longer on earth: but for a far older Christian tradition, its point is not that the Son of God is no longer on earth, but that the Son of Man is now in heaven. There is a human being in heaven. Contrast Newman's melancholy about leave-taking with Pope Leo the Great's celebration:

> It was a great and indescribable cause for joy when, in the presence of the holy multitudes the nature of our human kind ascended above the dignity of all the heavenly creatures, rising above the angelic orders, above the sublimity of the archangels, with no limit amid the glory of heaven to the height of its ascent until, received into the company of the eternal Father, it was made sharer of the throne of his glory to whose nature it was united in the Son.
>
> Therefore, since the Ascension of Christ is our uplifting, rejoice and be glad. For on this day not only are we made certain heirs of paradise, but in Christ we have already reached the heights of heaven and obtained more abundant gifts through the favour of Christ than ever we lost by the malice of the devil.

But what does that actually mean? We need to get past the picture language. St Leo tells us that Christ is placed above the angels, and it would be easy to think of this in terms of some absurd court scene, in which Christ takes ceremonial precedence over androgynous figures in feathers and nightshirts. For the people of the ancient world to say that a human being took precedence over angels was to say something very different, very immediate, and very amazing. We think of angels as benign fictions, God's domestic staff. For St Leo, as for St Paul, angels were as often malign as benevolent: they were the elemental powers who ruled the world – who made the winds to blow and the stars to turn in their courses, who presided over the rise and fall of nations, war and famine and disease, who made good and bad luck. They represented everything that bears down on human beings, all the forces that constrain and defeat us. Death was an angel. And men and women were and are subject to the angels, to the great forces which enslave us, though nowadays we don't often call them angels: to blind inexorable economic forces, to ideologies, to the coercive power of the state, to the consuming energies within our own natures which divide us and make us less than human – angels of greed or violence or disordered appetite.

The Ascension proclaims our freedom from all this, and calls us to claim that freedom, to recover a humanity which is not a victim in the grip of blind forces. The Ascension doesn't empty the earth; it empties the heavens, by casting down the angels. The great silence that falls upon the earth at the Ascension is the stilling of the wing-beats of the immortals. Their time is over. There is a man in heaven, and men and women are no longer to bow down to angels or to empires. There are no gods, only the children of the living God, brothers and sisters of the proper man, who wishes us to be free. If we gaze into the heavens we will see nobody, only Jesus.

The body of Christ risen, ascended, glorified, is not some supernatural thing parked in some heavenly waiting-room for the next act in a sky spectacular: the Resurrection is not in its essence a doctrine about another world. It is an affirmation of the supreme value of this world, the world we live in. The risen body of Christ is here and now, your body and my body, revealed in its beauty wherever human beings are allowed to flourish and to be what God wills them to be, present in society in every attempt, however inadequate, to make of human community not some coercive uniformity, but a space in which people in their individuality and their vulnerability are given space and support. We glimpse this identity of our individual and communal identity with Christ every time we come to the Eucharist. It is your own mystery which is laid upon the table, St Augustine says. It is to the reality of what you are that you say Amen. Be what you see, receive what you are.

Tonight we have recalled our own roots as a College by sharing the worship of a Benedictine community. The Benedictine life itself represents a taming of angels. The earliest monks tried to live the lives of angels: swept away by zeal for the Gospel, they imagined a life utterly different from the ordinary life of other human beings, a life in which spirit was everything, body nothing. They wanted nothing more to do with the earth, but gazed and gazed into heaven. It was a movement which threatened to turn the Gospel itself into a consuming energy which flattened ordinary men and women, which dwarfed and trivialized the world in which men and women married and had children and worried about the cost of the next meal. The achievement of Benedict was to take that heroic, but inhuman, lifestyle and to bring it under the rule of sanctified common sense: in place of lonely heroes – or fanatics – wrestling with their demons in the wilderness, he set the ideal of an ordered human community, ruled by charity and mutual care, giving the world a glimpse of what a really human community might look like. He called his monks to contemplation, to an attentive concentration on God in prayer and study. But he understood, as no monastic founder had understood, the need to take account of the fact that we are men, not angels, and that love of God involves a loving attentiveness not only to God, but to the Creation, and to the world of men and women. And under his *Rule*, monasticism, instead of trivializing or devaluing the life of the world of ordinary men and women, became a source of renewal and enrichment for that world. Out of the Benedictine contemplation of God in his Word and his works there emerged, in the fullness of time, the Universities. What we do, and what our Benedictine predecessors did five hundred years ago, are each in their ways a celebration of the creating life of God in the world he has redeemed. And just as much as Benedict's monasteries, we need to try to ensure that this community in which we try to learn and to tell the truth about the way the world is, is a place where human beings can truly flourish, where their humanity – risen with Christ and seated at the right hand of God – will be nourished and enhanced. The *Rule* of St Benedict ends with a prayer for the monastery which might just as well be a prayer for a College:

Let them bear with weaknesses, whether of body or of character, with tolerant patience. Let them vie with one another in showing mutual obedience. Let no one follow what is useful for himself, but what is of use to another. Let them cherish mutual love, as brethren do. Let them fear God lovingly. Let them put absolutely nothing before Christ, and may he bring us all, together, to life eternal.

10

A sermon for Christ the King

Magdalen College Chapel, 2004
Readings: 1 Kgs 1; Rev. 1

It is always daunting to have to preach on a text from the
Book of Revelation, because Revelation is the most
bizarre book in the Bible. In fact, the Church took nearly
four hundred years to make up its mind whether or not it
should be allowed into the Bible at all, and to this day the
Eastern Orthodox Churches, although they recognize it as
part of Scripture, never read from it in their services.
Luther wanted to exclude it from the German New
Testament because he thought it encouraged nutters, and
it is the only book of the Bible that Calvin didn't write a
commentary on. In modern times, a string of writers from
George Bernard Shaw to D.H. Lawrence have denounced
it as the ramblings of a drug addict, or a dangerous psy-
chotic nightmare. A few years ago an enterprising Scottish
publishing firm issued pocket-sized editions of individual
books of the Bible at a pound apiece, with introductions
by famous authors. The edition of the Book of Revelation
had an introduction by Will Self, in which he blamed it

for the death of a friend, a paranoid schizophrenic who killed himself after reading it.

But the passage we heard tonight is one of the milder parts of the Book of Revelation, and I am daunted for a different reason. I am daunted because *both* our readings invite us to reflect on the religious significance of monarchy. The passage we heard in the second lesson, describing Jesus Christ as 'prince of the Kings of the earth', is also read in the Roman Catholic Church as part of the liturgy for the Feast of Christ the King. The first reading from the First Book of Kings is an extract from a much longer account of the succession of Solomon to the throne of his father David. And when I discovered what the readings for tonight were, my first instinct was to ask the Dean of Chapel to change them.

This is in part a purely personal difficulty: I was raised in a strongly Republican family in a rather notorious border town in Ireland in the 1950s, and though I've lived relatively harmlessly in England for more than forty years and am by instinct a conservative man, I have never entirely shaken off that inherited discomfort with kings and queens. But the difficulty is only partly mine, for the writers of both the Old and the New Testaments themselves have a bit of a problem with monarchy.

Consider the account of the succession of Solomon, which we heard part of in the first reading. David the King had grown old and feeble, and had ceased to lead his people. Lingering in his palace, his blood had grown thin, and he couldn't get warm. And so his councillors searched the length and breadth of the land for a nubile virgin to tend him: they came up with the gorgeous Abishag the Shunammite. She was instructed to look after *all* the King's needs, to share his bed, to lie in his bosom. But this enterprising attempt to fan the dying embers of the King's manhood failed: so desperate was the King's state that he simply couldn't respond to Abishag's delicious ministrations. As the writer tells us, 'The damsel was very fair, and cherished the King, and ministered to him: but the King knew her not.'

The King's impotence is a symbol of the disorder of Israel: the people drift leaderless, and at last one of David's many sons, Adonijah the son of Haggith, seized power and proclaimed himself king. He didn't bother to consult the senile David, and he pointedly excluded also the inner circle of David's court: Zadok the Priest, Nathan the Prophet, and above all David's favourite son, Solomon, and Solomon's mother, Bathsheba, the wife of Uriah the Hittite, whom David had murdered in order to possess her. David long ago had promised Bathsheba that her son, their son, would be king after him. Now, panic-stricken by Adonijah's coup and their own exclusion, the court clergy reproached David and demanded the fulfillment of his promise. And the King, peeved by Adonijah's presumption and stirred by his old love for Bathsheba, at last roused himself to action: he had Solomon escorted to the royal shrine of Gihon on the royal mule, which is the equivalent of giving him a palace stretch limo with the flags flying, and there Zadok the Priest and Nathan the Prophet anointed Solomon king, and placed him on the throne of his father David.

We did not in fact hear the finish of this story, but as
you might expect, it all ended badly for Adonijah: out-
manoeuvred by Nathan, Zadok and Solomon, Adonijah
takes sanctuary at the altar, refusing to budge from the
holy place until Solomon agrees to spare his life. But
though he pretends to accept his kid brother Solomon's
sovereignty, Adonijah in fact can't let go his longing to be
king, and eventually he tries a trick of his own. He persuades the gullible queen mother, Bathsheba, to ask
Solomon to let Adonijah marry Abishag the Shunamite, as
a sort of consolation prize. Solomon of course sees
through this ploy, even if his mother does not: in ancient
Israel, possession of a dead king's last wife or concubine
would greatly strengthen Adonijah's claim to the throne.
And for Solomon, this is the last straw, or maybe just the
excuse he has been waiting for: he finds a hitman and has
Adonijah murdered, and now he can sleep easy, the
unchallenged King of Israel. It is as if beneath this story of
struggle for domination runs a more ancient tale, the story
of Cain and Abel: the steps of Solomon's throne are
cemented with the blood of his brother Adonijah.

Sexual intrigue, violence, plot and counter-plot, the
manipulation of love and royal status for sordid personal
gain: how different, you might think, or at any rate till
recently you might have thought, how *very* different from
the home life of our own dear royal family. It's all a
wonderfully believable picture of the realities of monarchy: under the robes and trumpets, the anointing and the
acclamations, there is human nature, red in tooth and
claw, people doing other people down in order to

scramble to the top of the greasy pole. At the heart even of God's plan for Israel, there is human sin.

The compiler of the Book of Kings in fact believed that Solomon had been raised up by God to be King of Israel, and he praises him as wise above all other kings; but in this story he allows us to see the mechanisms of power at their bleakest: monarchy as conquest, the struggle of the strong and cunning for possession of the spoils; and as Adonijah finds to his cost, it is a struggle to the death. So it is a piquant irony that this story, so full of human craftiness and murderously ferocious competitiveness, should be preserved in Handel's glorious Coronation Anthem, used at every coronation since 1725: as if to remind us that under the robes and razzmatazz, human societies are always compromised by sin, that power is never innocent.

This is a world which John, the author of the Book of Revelation, would have recognized at once. He calls the risen Jesus 'King', and the 'King of Kings': his book is saturated with images of royal power and in it the figure of the exalted Christ is ablaze with light, surrounded by bewildering and frightening symbols of power and dominion – two-edged swords, trumpets, crowns, golden robes, lampstands. But John and his first readers were no admirers of monarchy, and in ascribing royalty to Jesus they were being quite consciously subversive: John was attacking, not exalting, earthly rule and earthly rulers.

John wrote from exile and imprisonment sometime in the 80s or 90s of the first century. The Emperor Domitian had been alarmed by the rapid growth of the Christian movement, whose members refused the ultimate loyalty

to the state symbolized by burning incense to the emperor,
a refusal which Domitian thought was sapping the unity
and strength of the empire. He launched a savage persecution against the Church, and the gaols and the execution places were crammed with his victims. So John's
book is a dense and bitter code in which the Roman
Empire and the Roman Emperor, the supreme repre-
sentatives of earthly rule, are portrayed, not as the legitimate enforcers of law and order, ordained by God and
duly to be obeyed, which is what Paul says in the Letter to
the Romans, but as the enemies of God: Babylon the
Great, the Beast, the Antichrist. Christ is called King of
Kings in John's book because that is what Domitian
claimed to be, and all the details of his vision are a reversal
of the blasphemous claims of the Roman state to total
allegiance. The Emperor demanded that all the people of
his empire worship him as their lord and god, and a special
day of veneration had been created for this purpose – the
Emperor used the title *Kurios*, Lord, and this day of royal
veneration was called the Lord's day. On his coinage
Domitian is portrayed, as Christ appears here in this first
chapter of Revelation, with seven stars in his hand.

So to call Christ King was to deny that Domitian was
king: the Lordship of Christ was for John a rejection of the
idolatrous claims of the powers of his age, which he saw as
entirely evil, doomed to be overthrown by the imminent
return of King Jesus. But what a King: the mighty Lord of
the universe was not a conquering emperor, but a
slaughtered lamb; it is not power which sits enthroned at
the heart of the universe, but meekness. Whatever the

appearances in our world, John believed that God was on the side of the powerless and marginalized. The defeated and the victims were the truly blessed; death and destruction waited for the leaders of the big battalions.

John wrote in a time of persecution: he had urgent existential reasons for distrusting the powers of the state and the trappings of earthly power. For him the *Pax Romanum* was a hollow mockery, a demonic parody of what real human peace, real human community ought to be.

So John is a special case. But that same strand of distrust of earthly rule and earthly rulers runs through the New Testament, even in Paul, who was proud of his Roman citizenship and preached obedience to the powers that be; yet Paul, too, remembered that he preached a message incomprehensible to those whose hearts were set on power or domination. As he told the Corinthians,

> We speak wisdom, but not the wisdom of this world, nor of the princes of this world, that come to nothing. But we speak the wisdom of God in a mystery, which none of the princes of this world knew, for had they known it, they would not have crucified the Lord of Glory.'

For all the writers of the New Testament, the claim that Jesus was King was rooted not in a desire to legitimate or commend human political arrangements, but in savage irony, a commentary on the mocking and murder of the Son of God by the combined rulers of Israel and Rome. Christ's first and defining proclamation as King was a sick joke, nailed to his cross: Jesus of Nazareth, King of the Jews; and when he was revealed to the people, crowned with thorns and robed in purple, they did not shout, as in Handel's Anthem, 'Long live the king, may the king live for ever,' but 'Crucify him: *we* have no king but Caesar.'

The nations must be ruled: we have to have government, and maybe monarchy is no worse a form of government than any other. We need our symbols, and kings and queens can be powerful symbols. In the time of King David they were symbols of God's direct involvement in Israel's life, visible shepherds and guardians reflecting God's care of his flock; in our own not so remote past they were symbols of the power and pride of the people, the king's triumphs were our triumphs, the king's enemies our enemies: confound their knavish tricks, frustrate their politics. In modern times, they have made themselves symbols of less ferocious values, with the royal family represented as the ultimate happy family.

We have all been unwilling witnesses to the bitter unravelling of all of that, and the lip-smacking relish with which the media delight to expose the human frailty under the ermine robes. There is no ultimate happy family, and no human being can carry for long the weight of our projected hopes and imagined perfections. Every idol has feet of clay, or at any rate of flesh and blood.

And as with kings, so with kingdoms: all human government falls short of the ideals for which government is supposed to exist – fairness, compassion, the just distribution of the world's resources, the protection of the weak, the containment of the strong. All leadership, however well-intentioned, is liable to be contaminated by the desire to dominate, and by personal ambition; all forms of service constantly slide into modes of power.

The kingdom of Jesus is based, in John's words, in brotherhood and companionship and tribulation: the Son of Man has endured all that human beings can do to one another in hate, and has emerged utterly without hate, urgent to heal and rescue those who have hated him. He knows what is in our hearts; he knows and has suffered the worst that we are, the worst that we can do, and he loves us still. The keys of death and hell which he holds are not to lock us in, but to liberate us from the cycle of domination and struggle and murderous rivalry which dogs our history and shadows even our noblest aspirations and shared institutions. To accept his rule is to enter into the perfect freedom of love, to align ourselves not with the powerful but with the powerless, to seek to make all the structures of our own society and our own community instruments of care, not instruments of domination. Earthly thrones are built on fear and the power to over-awe; distance is part of their meaning; kings and queens have subjects. But Christ the King has no subjects, only brethren, loved, free, and summoned to put aside all fear – fear of life, fear of death, fear of one another, fear of the forces which control and distort and frustrate our lives. The crowds on Good Friday shouted 'We have no king but Caesar', we are invited tonight to say, 'We have no King but Jesus Christ.'

11

A sermon for St Mary Magdalene

Magdalene College Cambridge, 2003
John 20: 11–18

If you look up the chapel to the East window, you'll see the story we heard in the Gospel tonight, vividly illustrated by Augustus Welby Pugin. There it is in the far right-hand panel, with all the expected details. Pugin has even put Jesus into fancy dress with a rake in his hand so that we understand the nature of Mary's confusion – she supposes him to be the gardener.

In all the stories of Jesus' resurrection appearance to Mary Magdalene, she is the first witness to the risen Lord, *Apostola Apostolorum*, the Apostle to the Apostles. Jesus has not yet shown himself to any of the apostles; his Resurrection so far has been nothing but an impossible dream, a deduction which nobody dares to make from the brute fact of the empty tomb, 'For as yet they knew not the Scripture, that he must rise again from the dead.' In John's account of that Easter dawn, the mother of all the hopeful mornings of the world, there are, to begin with, no angels in shining garments. There are just the shocking facts of an empty grave and a bundle of soiled linen. In all the other

Gospels, the women encounter angels as soon as they arrive at the tomb, they are told by them to break the good news of the Resurrection to the apostles, and they duly rush away. But there agreement ends. Mark tells us that they said nothing to anyone, because they were afraid; Matthew says that they hurried off to deliver the message as they had been instructed, meeting Christ himself along the way. In tonight's Gospel, Peter and John come running to check the facts of Mary's testimony for themselves; Luke, by contrast, thinks the apostles took no notice, because the women's words 'seemed unto them as idle tales, and they believed them not'. It's all very confusing.

In John's story, in any case, we have to ask ourselves what Mary is *doing* at the tomb. Nice girls in first-century Palestine didn't walk around alone in the dark outside the city walls, even on a Sunday. For Luke and Mark the answer is straightforward: Mary Magdalene is not a nice girl, she's a spice girl. She is part of a little cluster of women who formed Jesus' groupies or fan-club, paying his bills, and cooking and washing for him as he travelled around the country preaching. They have evidently been with him from the start of his mission in Galilee, because Magdala, Mary's home town, is a fishing village in Galilee. And she and her women friends have a perfectly good reason for seeking out the grave as dawn breaks. Because the Sabbath began as night fell on Good Friday, Jesus had been hastily buried, with none of the normal washing and anointing of the corpse; so now, at the earliest possible opportunity, bringing the necessary ointments and spices,

the women who cared for him in life have come to per-
form one last service to the body of their executed teacher.

But not in our reading. That jar of ointment in Mary's
hand in Pugin's stained-glass rendering of tonight's story
has wandered in from the other Gospels, and strictly
speaking it has no business here at all. According to John,
Jesus didn't need to be anointed on Easter morning,
because his body had already been anointed on Good
Friday. John tells us that Jesus' corpse was prepared
according to Jewish custom, by two secret disciples,
Joseph of Arimathea and Nicodemus, who provide the
shroud and a huge hundred-weight batch of mixed ointment in which they wrap him.

That jar of ointment is Mary Magdalene's logo, her
emblem: she carries it or has it by her in almost every
picture ever painted of her, and you can see it there in
each of the five panels of our window. In fact, she carries
ointment not just and not mainly because ointment is
mentioned in the Resurrection stories, but because,
throughout the Middle Ages, the Church mixed her up
with an entirely different woman. And that mix-up has
persisted. The Anthem the choir sang tonight tells the
story of an encounter between Jesus and a weeping
woman with a jar of ointment. It's often used on feasts of
our saint, but as a matter of fact the story it tells, which
you can see there in the left-hand panel of the window,
has nothing whatever to do with Mary Magdalene. In one
form or another it occurs in all four Gospels. In Matthew
and Mark, the story takes place in the days leading up to
the Crucifixion, and the woman is just an anonymous

woman, who expresses her devotion to Jesus by anointing his head while he is at a formal dinner-party, breaking open an expensive alabaster jar of scented ointment to do it. When the Apostles complain that the ointment could have been sold for charity, Jesus says there will be time enough for looking after the poor, and interprets the gesture as a prophecy of his death: this woman will be remembered for ever because her extravagant action foretells his burial.

Luke's version is very different, for in it the anonymous woman has become a woman of the town, and a great sinner – the implication is probably that she is a prostitute, and that she's carrying that scented ointment to excite her clients. She anoints Jesus' feet, not his head, and not only with ointment but with her tears, which she wipes away with her hair. Nice girls didn't massage men's feet with perfume in public; and they didn't let down their hair either. And so Jesus' unbelieving host, Simon the Pharisee, is scandalized by all this body contact: if Jesus were really what he claims to be, he would know exactly what this woman was, and he wouldn't endure her touch. But Jesus turns the incident into a lesson about love: throughout the Gospels he deliberately breaks the taboos that put people beyond the pale – the laws about ritual purity that surrounded leprosy for example, or menstruating women. Jesus sweeps aside these barriers, quite literally reaching out to people, touching them or letting them touch him. And so it is in the story of the prostitute with the ointment – the touch of this sinner is no defilement, but the gesture of a heart overcome with love. Simon's ungenerous self-righteousness is the sign of a clenched and shrivelled heart, whereas 'Her sins, which are many, are forgiven her, for she loved much: but to whom little is forgiven, the same loveth little.'

Luke's version became the canonical form of the story, and it is not hard to see why: the penitent prostitute with the tumbling hair is a pretty exciting notion, especially if you're a painter; that's why pictures of Mary Magdalene, including the ones in our window, often dress her in gorgeous clothes. Admittedly, Pugin's Mary Magdalene is a fairly prim figure, but more commonly she is portrayed as deliberately voluptuous: somewhere in all that glamorous finery, you are meant to think, there is probably a large and enticing zip.

There's more than the picturesque or the salacious at work here. Luke's version of the story of the woman with the ointment has a depth and tenderness lacking in all the other Gospels, and it is the same tenderness which we see in our Johannine Resurrection story. But John's story is a sort of reversal of Luke's. There is no doubting Mary's love for Jesus: she has stood by the cross when most of the Apostles had run away, and now she is here before dawn to weep for him. Just that: there is no work to be done, except the work of love. Her tears flow, desolation breathes in all her words: 'They have taken away the Lord, and we know not where they have laid him. Sir, if thou hast borne him hence, tell me where thou hast laid him, and I will take him away.'

But as yet this love lacks vision: it's earthbound, and the interchange between Jesus and Mary, for all its pathos, is a test. Like the apostles, she has failed in faith, she is blind to the stupendous reality of life standing there in front of her. Despite the evidence of her own eyes, she mistakes the living Jesus for a gardener, and seeking her Lord she looks only for a corpse. And so, with the same distancing, impersonal word which he used to his uncomprehending mother at the marriage feast at Cana, Jesus distances the unbelieving Mary – '*Woman*, why weepest thou, whom seekest thou?' And then intimacy is restored to this frosty interchange, in one of the most touching moments in the Gospels, with a single word. In reply to Mary's cry of desolation, '*Tell* me where thou hast laid him,' Jesus says only her name: 'Mary.' God shows himself to us by showing us first who we are: we do not know him, until he calls us by our name.

It's part of the magnificence of John's art and insight, however, that even after this moment of recognition, Mary is kept at arm's length, unlike the prostitute in the other story. Impetuously she throws herself at Jesus, but touch me not, he says, *Noli me tangere*, for I am not yet ascended to my father.

Why can't she touch him? He's real enough: the tomb is empty, this is no ghost or vision. One week on, when he appears on this Sunday, Low Sunday, to Thomas, he will actually invite him to insert a finger into his wounds. The commentators all agree that we are being told here that Resurrection life transcends earthly affections: Jesus' death has put an end to the old intimacies, so Mary must wait for the Pentecostal gift which will replace physical closeness with something far better, the shared life of the Spirit, which makes all who love and follow Christ the children of God, as he, uniquely, is the child of God. His God will become their God in a new and unimaginable way.

But painters have been just as fascinated by this scene as the theologians have, and they have seen other possibilities. One of the most marvellous of all evocations of our story is a painting in the National Gallery, Titian's *Noli me Tangere*, painted in 1512. The risen Jesus, an almost naked vision of perfect manhood, stands bathed in the golden and blue light of an idyllic dawn landscape, spring foliage burgeoning all around him. Sprawled in shadow on the ground before him, a deliciously plump Mary Magdalene, her hair and clothes tumbled loosely around her, reaches a hand longingly towards him, emphatically of the earth. And Jesus, gracefully, kindly, but inexorably, curvettes away from her touch. Of course the picture illustrates John's story, perfectly; but it also offers an unforgetable this-worldly message, a meditation on the paradoxes of desire, intensified by abstinence, liable to be spoiled or disappointed by experience and satiety.

The figure of Mary Magdalene has been taken to symbolize many things in Christian history: the penitent sinner seeking forgiveness of sin; the superiority of the spiritual over the material; even the mortified life of monks and nuns. All impecably conventional morals, and some or all of these must have been in the mind of our founders when they chose her as our patron saint. But the Magdalene is also a subversive figure, reaching out to touch the untouchable, an insistent reminder of the claims of the earthly in the midst of the spiritual, a woman who teaches the apostles. And maybe that last aspect of our story is the most subversive of all. It's ironic, I think, that Cambridge's only College dedicated to the first woman teacher of Christianity, the Apostle of the Apostles, should have been the last to admit women as teachers and students. Her role as teacher worried medieval commentators: how could a woman have evangelized the apostles, when St Paul had expressly forbidden them to speak of sacred things? But for all the worries, that aspect of Mary Magdalene surfaces time and again: she is often depicted in medieval art in the act of preaching, and she was even credited in the Middle Ages with having evangelized the south of France. So maybe that's what we should take away from tonight's story: that the College of Mary Magdalene should be a place where human tenderness and spiritual vision go together; that we should cherish each other, call each other by name; and that we should try not to be blinded by prejudice and status, and be ready to listen and learn from anyone who can teach us.

12

The formidable finger:
St John the Baptist

Oxford University, 2005
John 1: 35–7

Heatstroke in London parks and tropical rainstorms in Glastonbury are not exactly evocative of Christmas. Yet today's commemoration of John the Baptist is in fact firmly tied to Christmas Day. As far back as Christian calendars go, 24 June has been observed as the major feast day of the Baptist, his nativity. By and large, the Christian calendar doesn't take any notice of the natural birthdays of the saints. It's their heavenly birthdays, the day of their deaths, which we commemorate. But although the Church does also commemorate the beheading of the Baptist, on 29 August, for John, even more than for Jesus, the birthday is the thing.

It's not hard to see why. St Luke's Gospel opens with the story of two miraculous conceptions and births, Jesus and John. Both boys are conceived by impossible mothers – a Virgin and a barren, old-age pensioner – both are announced by angels and surrounded by heavenly signs. And the angel Gabriel, in the story of the Annunciation, fixes precisely for us the birthday of the Baptist: he tells

Mary that Elizabeth, her cousin, is pregnant in her old age, and 'This is the sixth month with her who was called barren.' So John is just six months older than Jesus: they divide the year between them. And once the birthday of Jesus became fixed in Christian tradition at the winter solstice on 25 December, then the Church had a date for John's birthday too, 24 June, at the summer solstice.

The Christians of late antiquity loved symbolic correspondences and symmetries, and the stories of Jesus and John, especially in St Luke's Gospel, are full of them. Two angelic Annunciations, two impossible births, two specially revealed names, two canticles, the *Magnificat* and the *Benedictus*, sung by Jesus' mother and John's father, and so on. Jesus appears in the dead of winter, John in high summer. From John's birthday onwards the days begin to shorten, the darkness begins to lengthen: from Jesus' birthday onwards the days begin to lengthen, the light begins to grow. Ancient commentators saw a link here to the passage in St John's Gospel, where the Baptist says of Jesus, 'He must increase, I must decrease.' They liked to dwell on the fact that this contrast was gruesomely true of the deaths of John and Jesus, as well as of their mission and lives – John decreased quite literally, since he had his head chopped off, whereas Jesus increased because he was raised high on a cross. But the symmetry was most obvious in that natural pattern of the year. From John's birth, the days dwindle towards darkness; from Jesus's birth, the days stretch towards the light. And Zacharias, John's father, says to his newborn son,

And thou child shalt be called the prophet of the
Highest: for thou shalt go ahead of the Lord to
prepare his ways,
To give knowledge of salvation unto his people, for
the remission of their sins,
Through the tender mercy of our God: whereby the
day spring from on high hath visited us,
To give light to them that sit in darkness, and the
shadow of death.

So John, then, is a figure of the darkness before the dawn:
he stands at the cusp of the morning just as he stands at the
mid-point of the year. For St Luke, of course, all this talk
of day and night had a deeper symbolic resonance. The
pre-dawn dusk in which John's mission is to be carried out
stands for the partial revelation of the Old Covenant. It's
not a coincidence that John's father and mother are *ancient*,
or that John's father is a priest of the old order, the servant
of that Temple which was soon to pass away. Zacharias
represents religion as formality, religion as ritual and
sacrifice; and he is rendered dumb by his inability to
believe the promises announcing the new age of the Spirit
which is to come. In fact, everyone we meet there in the
Temple – Simeon, Anna, Zacharias himself, all of them
are *old*. John himself represents religion as renunciation
and discipline, religion at its most demanding; but he too
comes at the end of the age, he's the last of the prophets of
the Old Testament. Dressed like Elijah in camel hair and
leather belt, John is the last voice of warning and vigilant

longing, before the desire of the ages himself appears, and
the world's long time of expectation comes to an end.

For John doesn't just stand at the dividing line between
night and day. He forms the divide between two cove-
nants, between the old order and the new. St Augustine
says that John stands *quidam limes . . . veteris et novi*, 'Like a
sort of threshold between the old and the new'. John is
born to be the man at the edge, the man on the outside
looking in. On the outside, because as soon as he is old
enough to walk, he takes himself off into the wilderness,
the great outdoors. St Luke tells us that 'The child [John]
grew and became strong in the spirit, and he was in the
wilderness till the day of his manifestation to Israel.' And
he remains a figure of the wilderness, the dangerous edge;
he is, as all the Gospels tell us, 'A voice crying in the
wilderness, make straight the way of the Lord.' When he
began to preach, Mark tells us, 'John the Baptizer appeared
in the wilderness, . . . and there *went out to him* all the
country of Judaea, all the people of Jerusalem.'

So John doesn't just stand on the threshold between the
old and new order of things, or at the cusp between
darkness and day; he also stands at the edge between the
city and the desert, and between what city and desert stand
for – between the safe boundaries of the known, and the
dangerous edge of things, between meaning and chaos. To
hear what he has to say, you have to go out to him, you
have to make an effort, take a risk. In medieval painting he
is often depicted in this way, as what the Irish call a
mountainy man, raw-boned, hairy, gaunt, wild-eyed,
barefoot: the figure who stands in the foreground of

Grünewald's Isenheim Altarpiece, pointing with bony finger to the tormented body of the crucified. Jesus' own contemporaries were alert to all this, they saw that this wildness and austerity made John utterly different to Jesus; for John stayed outside the towns, eating and drinking nothing except those awful locusts, while Jesus went where the crowds were, he was a wine-bibber and a glutton according to his enemies, constantly partying with unsuitable people, like us. And when Jesus submitted himself to John's baptism, he himself was driven out into the wilderness, to live with the wild beasts and to be tempted by demons. John stands not just for the rigorist demands of religion, then, but for danger, for the threatening emptiness just outside the boundaries of the known, for the wild beasts and the wasteland beyond the city wall, and for those other wastelands of the heart and mind, in which the beasts roam and the boundaries are lost.

And the wilderness John inhabits is a wilderness on the move. It threatens to invade, to break down the walls of our securities. John announces desolation and destruction to the city, he represents a power that can turn the garden into a wilderness. 'Flee from the wrath to come,' he announces in St Matthew's Gospel, 'Even now the axe is laid to the root of the trees.'

The first Christians found all this less disconcerting than most of us are likely to do, because for them there was more to the wilderness than emptiness and fear. The desert was the place where Israel encountered God, it was the place of revelation. That's why John had gone there at all, and why the Spirit drove Jesus there once John had baptised him. In fact, from about the fourth century, Christian commentators saw John as the prototype and patron of all those who deliberately went out into the wilderness in order to find God: John the Baptist, they thought, was the first monk, and his message of repentance and purification made sense to them. They believed that you could fling away comfort and security and still have a meaningful and dignified existence; in fact, they thought it was easier to find meaning and dignity without security: the walls of the city, they recognized, were often designed to keep God – and our own humanity – securely locked out or locked up.

For us, it is different. We feel the threat and the desolation of the empty spaces. It's harder for us to believe that in and through them there might be meaning and renewal and rebirth; it's hard for us to believe that the mountainy man has a hidden wisdom, or can be anything other than a skeleton at the feast. In his inauguration sermon in April 2005, Pope Benedict XVI reflected on this widespread feeling of desolation and threat, humanity confronted with the wilderness of a world without meaning. He said,

> So many people are living in the desert. And there are so many kinds of desert. There is the desert of poverty, the desert of hunger and thirst, the desert of abandonment, of loneliness, of destroyed love. There is the desert of God's darkness, the emptiness of souls no longer aware of their dignity or the goal of human

life. The external deserts in the world are growing, because the internal deserts have become so vast.

The new Pope believes that humanity in the twenty-first century has wandered into a desert of inanity, a wasteland, in which death is merely the last pointless happening in a chain of pointless events. And while he was still Cardinal Ratzinger, he explained to his fellow-Cardinals on the eve of the Conclave just what he meant by this desert of the human spirit, the shifting rootless disorientation of a humanity,

> tossed from one extreme to the other, from Marxism to liberalism, from collectivism to radical individu-alism, from atheism to a vague religious mysticism . . . What is being constructed is a dictatorship of relati-vism, which recognizes nothing as definitive, and that regards one's self and one's desires as the ultimate measure.

The Pope's remedy, like John's, is the announcement of the demanding but still good news that there is in fact a highway through the wilderness: the way of Christ, clear and straight, running for all to see, in the faith and practice of the Church. Behold the Lamb of God. 'We, however,' declared Cardinal Ratzinger, 'have another measure: the Son of God, the true man. He is the measure for true humanity, the criterion for discerning between the true and the false, between deception and truth. We must mature in this adult faith, and it's towards this faith that we must lead the flock of God.'

This is a precious affirmation, and many people within the Catholic Church and beyond it look forward to receiving from this Pope, as from the last, clear and firm teaching, a steer away from confusion and relativism, and the assurance that there is indeed for us a highway through the wilderness. Well and good: we need to hear such assurances. But in making them, there's a danger of imagining that the desert has been safely banished once we find faith in God. There is a kind of triumphalism, a cosmic cosiness, in emphasizing too much the contrast between the bewilderment, cluelessness and despair of humanity without faith on the one hand, and confident Christian clarity and hope on the other. But John and the wilderness he brings with him is not a figure of the past, or a warning for other people. He is the embodiment of a recurrent reality in the experience even of people of faith. He was indeed a voice announcing the presence of the Word – *behold the Lamb of God*; but he himself lived with questions and uncertainties, even about Jesus: he sent his disciples to Jesus to ask, are you he who is to come, or should we look for another? Cardinal Ratzinger's contrast between the relativism of the secular world and the saving certainties of the Church was gently but firmly nuanced, perhaps even corrected, a few weeks after the Conclave, in a sermon preached on the twenty-fifth anniversary of his ordination as a bishop by Cardinal Martini, formerly Archbishop of Milan. Taking as his theme the Last Judgement, Martini emphasized how inadequate and partial even the fundamental affirmations of Christianity are in that mysterious perspective; how provisional and imperfect even our deepest convictions are and ought to be in the face of the mystery of God and the tragedies of human existence. We are travellers on the highway; the wilderness is all around us; it is within us, to the journey's end; we travel in hope, not in certainty.

And in fact St Augustine himself used more than one of his sermons for the feast of St John to develop a contrast between the immense mystery of God on the one hand, and everything we have to say about him on the other. He liked to dwell on that phrase of John: 'I must decrease, he must increase.' John was, Augustine insisted, before everything else, a voice. When that voice was born, it put an end to the silence which had descended upon a religion faltering in its faith, in the person of the priest Zachary, John's father. But Augustine was intensely aware that the whole purpose of that voice was to speak a Word which was the ultimate communication, God's presence and his very self and essence all divine, in Newman's phrase, and yet which, though we call it the Word, is beyond all the resources of language. He reminds us that, in the end, there is nothing that can be adequately said about God, whose Word exceeds all the powers of all the voices which ever have sought, or can seek, to express it. In the end, John is greater than all the prophets, because he *doesn't* speak, he falls silent, and points, away from himself, towards the mystery: *behold the Lamb of God*. The Fathers and medieval commentators return again and again to that gesture of pointing: medieval relics of his finger multiplied, and behind that bogus multiplication lay a sound exegetical instinct, for John's pointing finger is the most important thing about him. It is as a man with a pointing finger that he is depicted again and again in Western art.

E.M. Forster has a dismissive aside somewhere about 'poor, talkative little Christianity'. And in preaching about John, Augustine repeatedly went out of his way to point out the limitations even of God-talk, of the voice, and its inferiority to the truths it has to utter. So, he says, 'Somebody groans: that's a voice. Someone wails: that's a voice. It's a formless sound, carrying a noise to the ears, but no meaning.' What passes for language is all too often nothing but noise. And even at best, all speech, he thinks, is noise organized towards an end, not important for what it is, but for what it points us towards. One day, we will have no need for the clumsy code of language, we will have no need for creeds, even for the Gospels themselves:

All voices must necessarily diminish, when we are promoted to seeing Christ. The more you make progress towards seeing wisdom, the less need you have of a voice. A voice in the prophets, a voice in the psalms, a voice in the apostles, a voice in the Gospel. But when we see him as he is, you don't suppose, do you, that the Gospel will be chanted? You don't imagine we will hear the prophecies, or read the letters of the apostles? Why not? Because the voices must fall away, as the Word grows, because he must grow, and I must decrease.

And the way beyond mere religious talk, beyond knowledge, to the silence of wisdom, lies still through the wilderness. The Baptist is the reminder that humanity is indeed beset by the desert, deserts outside us, and the greater deserts within. For many, perhaps for most of our contemporaries, and for many and perhaps for most of us, the world is indeed a wilderness, a dangerous and uncertain place: this is the human condition, the terror of finitude, the limitation of our vision, the certainty of our own mortality:

> The glacier knocks in the cupboard
> The desert sighs in the bed
> And the crack in the teacup opens
> A lane to the land of the dead:

Believers too journey through this wilderness of uncertainty: faith brings no immunity from the pain of being human. But the Baptist is a reminder also that through the wilderness of the world there does indeed run a road: a way to walk in hope, a direction to follow:

> In the deserts of the heart
> Let the healing fountain start.

Every day in the Mass there is a vivid reminder both of that journey through the wilderness, and of the assurance of journey's end: when the priest holds up the host before the communicants, he repeats John's words: *behold the Lamb of God, behold him who takes away the sins of the world.*

And he adds, 'Happy are those who are called to His Supper.' Many priests paraphrase that last sentence into a cosy reference to the present: 'Happy are we who are called to his holy table.' But the Supper referred to is not the Mass or the Lord's Supper, the service then going on. It is the great supper at the end of the Ages, the Marriage Supper of the Lamb, beyond time and circumstance, to which we hope but cannot know that we have been invited. Even there, even at the heart of the Mass, at the supreme moment of affirmation, with the sacramental presence of the Lamb of God before our eyes and within our reach, even there we stand alongside John in the wilderness, and are reminded by him that the desire of the ages, the resolution of our uncertainties and the consolation of our longings, lies still ahead, along the line of that formidable finger.

13

The terrible joys:
St Valentine's Day

Great St Mary's, Cambridge, 1984

Next door to the school in which I spent my adolescence was a large baroque church: all round the aisles were side chapels and confessionals, arranged alternately – confessional, chapel, confessional, chapel. Twice a term or so there were compulsory school Masses, and before each Mass the exceptionally pious or the notoriously wicked assembled in sheepish and slightly apprehensive rows to go to Confession. One of the priests there was an unwordly man well known for his tolerance of schoolboy peccadilloes, and we flocked in droves to his box, leaving the good Fathers on either side to while away the time by saying the rosary or reading the newspapers behind the curtains of their untenanted confessionals.

The chapel nearest this busy box had a glass-fronted altar. Behind the glass lay a dusty gilt casket with the legend *Sanctus Valentinus*, and I often wondered how the bones of this shadowy Roman martyr, about whom nothing very much is known, ended up under the murky skies of Birmingham. I later found out: church and school had been founded by Cardinal Newman, and the relics of St Valentine were a gift to him from the Pope, brought, despite resistance from puzzled and suspicious port officials, to their resting place in the English Midlands.

It seems that Newman's St Valentine is not, in fact, the one we celebrate on 14 February; but those bones make a useful departure all the same for today's festival, because they highlight its oddity. St Valentine's Day is traditionally a celebration of the flesh, of the pairing of male and female, a spring festival before winter is fully gone, which celebrates the rising of the sap, the mating of bird and beast and human kind: nothing could be less otherworldly, and yet we keep this feast on the martyrdom day of an obscure Roman cleric with a beautiful name. Why?

Oddly enough, the answer, like the bones, is to be found here in England. It was all invented by Geoffrey Chaucer. Towards the end of the fourteenth century he composed his poem *The Parliament of Fowls*. This describes a dream he had on St Valentine's Day of a glorious, earthly paradise, a garden in which love and beauty rule. The garden is inhabited by the great lovers of the classical and Romance past – Cleopatra, Dido, Tristan and Isolde, Helen of Troy. But at the centre of the garden are gathered all the birds of the air, presided over by Nature herself. They have come to choose their mates. The bulk of the poem centres on the dilemma of a gentle tercel eagle who is wooed by two males – how is she to choose between them? The birds elect spokesmen to give their views: the cuckoo, duck and goose with the grossness and lack of feeling you would expect, the turtle dove with chivalry. The poem concludes with the more prosaic birds happily mated, but the high-minded eagles doomed to pine in celibacy for another year; and a chorus of song-birds hymn St Valentine:

> Saint Valentyn that art full *high* on loft
> Thus singen smalle fowles for thy sake,
> Now welcomee summer with thy sunne soft.
> That hast this winters wethers overtake.

Birds, flowers, spring in the air, the hint of romance: the combination proved irresistible. Chaucer's theme was picked up by other, duller, poets, and, within a few generations St Valentine's Day had become the recognized time for proposing marriage or sending love tokens; and the custom survives.

Hardly worth all this talk though, you might think, and not in any case in Christian worship. That's very possibly true; but I can't help feeling that it all goes to preserve for Christians a vital perspective on sexual love which the Church has sometimes shown itself unable or unwilling to come to terms with. That is, quite simply, the acceptance of the love between man and woman for what it first and foremost is, part of the instinctive drive of all created things to perpetuate themselves, the impersonal and animal force that links us with the brute creation, with bird and beast and flower. It's a force that shines, like God's sun, on just and unjust alike, our share in the overflowing creativity of nature. Organized Christianity has always been a bit embarrassed about it. The New Testament has virtually

nothing to say about it, and Christian thinkers have
repeatedly tried either to ban sex altogether, or to turn it
into something vaguely religious. At every wedding we're
reminded that the relation between husband and wife
represents that between Christ and his Church, and the
Song of Solomon, that most lush and unashamed celebration of physical love, only got into the canon of
Scripture heavily disguised as a mystical poem about Christ
and the Church or the soul and its God. Read the
Authorized Version of the first lesson we heard read today
and you will find that it is headed, 'The mutual love of
Christ and his Church.' I don't want to say that I think that
the love of man and woman has nothing to do with our
relationship with God, but only that as actully employed,
the metaphor has encouraged a false idealization of sexual
love which anyone who has experienced it knows to be
unreal. Even in a good marriage we are propelled into one
another's arms not by altruistic self-sacrifice, which is how
ideal marriage is sometimes presented, not least by St Paul,
but by a mixture of motives – by need, by habit, above all
by sheer enjoyment. In marriage, more than anywhere
else, we experience our own creatureliness, and this is as it
should be: human beings and not angels are the children of
God. The likeness of the sexual relationship to the love
between Christ and the Church does not mean its disem-
bodying, but recalls us to the wonder of the Incarnation.
God drew near to us not by evaporating flesh into Spirit,
but by lodging his Word and his wisdom in the flesh.

The last century or so has seen genuine attempts by the
Church to face up to the positive nature of sex. We no

longer care to talk of marriage as a concession to humanity's fallen nature, a moral alternative to burning. But the
resulting emphasis the other way has sometimes been
unfortunate, as anyone who has listened to what can only
be called the juicy language of some of the newer liturgies
of marriage can testify. And in the process, sexual love has
been sacralized, invested with a holy glamour. In the
1960s and 1970s there was a rash of embarrassing books by
liberalized priests and clericalized psychiatrists about
marriage and love which, in their idealization of sexual
love, struck many as every bit as unreal as the earlier
tradition of repression and constraint. Somehow, God had
crept into the bed, and one longed for the sanity of
Charles Williams' advice: 'When you play, don't pray, and
when you pray, don't play.'

But of course, it isn't as simple as that. The mating urge
links us to brute and bird, but our own divided nature
parts us from them. We are amphibious creatures: we
breathe the air of heaven as well as that of earth, hovering
like the eagle between flesh and spirit, not wholly at ease
in either. Alone of all the creatures, we stand back from
our headlong involvement in the cycle of birth and
copulation and death, and, in pledging our hearts, we
alone are capable of infidelity, of passing the limits of our
own loyalties. Alone of all the creatures we do not mate in
the innocence of Eden. For mankind alone, love is a life-
work which can make or destroy us. Chaucer's poem
begins with lines which are often quoted as if they referred
to the art of writing, but which in fact reflect on this aspect
of the love of man and woman:

> The life so short, the craft so long to learn,
> The array so hard, so sharp the conquering,
> The dreadful joy, always that flies so soon,
> All this mean I by love . . .

The vision of spring is part of our experience of love. Sex is the celebration of the flesh; it is, among much else, what the Church has never really wanted it to be, simply great fun. But we expect more than this from love, and must give more than this: on us is laid the burden and the glory of turning the mating instinct into a road to God, not by indulging in unreality, by romanticizing the mundane, by disguising our half-hearted commitment, by concealing the element of self-seeking and self-absorption which is an inescapable part of our relationships with one another, and above all of the sexual relationship. But rather, accepting all these limitations under grace, to shape within them a space in which love and trust can flourish, and the Spirit of Christ enter in. There is a fitting and instructive paradox, then, in celebrating the marriage of the flesh on a martyr's day, the paradox at the heart of the Gospel, proclaimed in the cross, that life can come only out of a willingness to die, that the self lives only in God's eye when self is surrendered to his will. For human beings, the careless joy of the birds on Valentine's Day can be purchased only with care, with loyalty, with another sort of love. Six hundred years after Chaucer, another Christian poet summed it up:

As I listened from a beach-chair in the shade
To all the noises that my garden made,
It seemed to me only proper that words
Should be withheld from vegetables and birds.

A robin with no Christian name ran through
The Robin-Anthem which was all it knew,
And rustling flowers for some third party waited
To say which pairs, if any, should get mated.

Not one of them was capable of lying,
There was not one which knew that it was dying
Or could have with a rhythm or a rhyme
Assumed responsibility for time.

Let them leave language to their lonely betters
Who count some days and long for certain letters;
We, too, make noises when we laugh or weep:
Words are for those with promises to keep.

[W. H. Auden, *Their Lonely Betters*]

14

Heavenly Jerusalem

Holy Trinity Church, Cambridge, in the presence of
the Lord Mayor, 2001

Readings: Rev. 21:10–22:5

Sometime towards the end of the first century, a Jewish–
Christian prophet named John wrote down his hopes for
the renewal of a broken world, the ending of sorrow and
the triumph of peace. We heard the result in the reading
from the Book of Revelation. It's a moving vision of the
heavenly city, the Jerusalem of his dreams. But the city of
John's vision is like no city on earth, for in it there is
neither sickness nor sorrow. It has no refuse or traffic
problems, no hospitals, or undertakers, or Citizens' Advice
Bureaux. It has no police either, for this is a city without
pimps or burglars, murderers or con men. By the same
token, John's holy city has no churches. John, of course,
was a Christian, but for him, as for Karl Marx eighteen
centuries later, organized religion was a symptom of
something wrong with the human race, the heart of a
heartless world. The need for churches was real, but it was
an ambulance measure, the unhappy consequence of our
distance from God and from one another. When that
estrangement is finally abolished, we won't need any

structures of intercession or appeal. There will be no temple. By contrast, because God lives in John's city, everything is free, there are no secrets and no exclusions. The building-bricks and paving slabs are translucent jewels, and its inhabitants have no fear of assault or invasion. Its gates are entrances, not barriers: they stand always open, and even asylum seekers are welcome.

John's vision is a mirror held up to our longings: and like all mirrors, it reflects back to us the reverse of reality. For us, the city is as likely to be a place of conflict and worry as of peace and security. Cambridge isn't an especially violent town, but even here you have to lock your door, your car, your bicycle; and the flocks of unhappy white-faced men and women with tin-whistles, dogs and drug or drink habits stationed at what sometimes seems every twenty or thirty yards along the streets make all the neediness and sadness of our world very plain indeed. Cities heave with life, but they heave with death too: in the midst of crowds, men and women are often terribly alone. In the city our callousness and indifference towards one another is most visible, our ability to brutalize and pollute our environment, our greed for gain and our disregard of consequences.

It's always been like that. John idealized Jerusalem and made it stand for the greatest freedoms and the highest hopes of humankind. But for him, another city represented everything in the human heart he most loathed and feared: tyranny, oppression, the silencing of truth and the murder of the innocent. He called that city Babylon, but he was using code, and his readers knew that he meant

Rome. When John was writing, Rome was the greatest city the world had ever known. All roads ran there, and it was the source of law and civilization: its courts and markets, libraries, and bath-houses epitomized everything that was gracious and life-enhancing, the best that human effort could achieve. But John wasn't impressed: he knew that all the splendour was built on blood: slave populations groaned to feed it, and those wonderful roads were designed to get the legions quickly to trouble-spots in the subjugated regions. And as he wrote, Rome was persecuting the Christian Gospel, and killing its preachers.

So for John, the power and organization of the greatest of earthly cities wasn't the pinnacle of civilization. It was the concentration of sin, a rerun of the rebellion of the tower of Babel, when human beings had organized themselves to storm heaven. In this version of things, the city is a criminal conspiracy, an attempt to declare a UDI (Unilateral Declaration of Independence) against God, to cheat death and time by our own unaided efforts.

Two cities, two visions: the city given by God as a place of harmony, hope, and mutual help, and the city constructed by men as a place of power and profit, where the weakest go to the wall. But Jerusalem and Babylon are in fact impossible to separate: vision and viciousness, good and evil, run through the heart of every human community, however sacred. For Christians, Jews and Muslims, Jerusalem is one of the earth's holiest places, it symbolizes the perfection and peace we all aspire to; its name fills our prayers and hopes:

If I do not remember thee, O Jerusalem, let my
tongue cleave to my mouth

but the recent savage history of the Holy Land, torn by the
twin evils of terrorism and oppression, reminds us of the
gulf between symbol and reality, and the fragility and
imperfection of all human communities.

The greatest Christian exploration of these issues is St
Augustine's great book, *The City of God*. In it, Augustine
argues that all human communities are defined by their
values, not their activities: you see what a community is
about by looking at what it *loves*. Every community is
made up of people united by a shared love. So the two
cities are expressions of two loves – love of God and other
people, or love of self. Jerusalem, and Babylon. Everyone
must choose which city they will be a citizen of, and those
opposite allegiances, to Jerusalem or Babylon, run and will
run through human history until the end of time, shaping
good and evil, making the actual communities we construct for ourselves either a haven or a hell.

We are what we love, and we are united to other
people by what we all love together. That's a wonderful
insight, but also a frightening one, because of course, for
us human beings, hate is the flip side of love. Brotherhood
almost always means otherhood, too, the rejection or
demonizing of those who *don't* fit in. Communities united
by a common bond – race or religion or ideology – are
often persecuting societies: medieval England was kept
Christian partly by killing or expelling anyone who wasn't
Christian, like the Jews. You only have to look at the

current history of the Balkans, or the Holy Land, to see how shared ideals and shared loyalties, defined over against other people, can become the excuse for murder and mayhem.

That's why many people nowadays would prefer to have cities *without* faith. They want a society where we each make our own values, which we don't impose on other people, or expect other people to share: provided no one suffers directly, live and let live. That sort of solution to the difficulties of living together goes back a long way. Since the seventeenth century, philosophers have often talked as if human societies were essentially armed truces between crowds of individuals: society is really sanctified selfishness. Everyone wants the best for themselves, but often the most efficient way to get the best for yourself is to join up with other people so that you can tackle jobs too big for one, like defending your property or building factories. Law in such a society isn't the expression of shared value, a common love, so much as a way of regulating people's existence alongside each other with the minimum of friction. The law should preserve as much individual freedom as is compatible with the efficient running of the system, and should leave private matters like religion, morality and value alone as much as possible.

In a world in which people find it harder and harder to agree about religion or morality, that's a tempting formula, and our society often acts on it. It is changing the texture of our lives together. Once upon a time, Britain was a uniformly Christian culture, and our laws and customs reflected that fact. Shops closed on Sundays, the major

Christian festivals were kept as holidays, the laws embodied Christian teaching on marriage and sexual morality, civic ritual and religious ceremonial were intertwined. Something of that historic relationship survives, indeed it's embodied in this very service: the mayor still comes to church. But everywhere, for good or ill, it is slipping. Walk round this city after 11am any Sunday, and it is a shopping day like any other. And the trend is more marked where other religious cultures are present and prominent. In Birmingham a few years ago, somebody decided there would be no Christmas lights, no public display of Christian symbols in December. The shopkeepers and council would put up bright lights to draw the shoppers in all right, but they must remove all the Christian emblems from them, and the December shopping and holiday period was called not Christmas, but 'Winterval'. Winterval lights. Birmingham was playing safe, opting for neutrality in public, keeping value and ideals for the private sphere, and in the process distancing itself from the Christianity which was its historical source of public value and symbolism. In place of a celebration of the new life of God coming to renew the world when all is dead and dark, all that was left was a shopping spree, and lights paid for by the shopkeepers to encourage people to come out and spend.

Is this the way forward for multi-ethnic, pluralist Britain? Maybe; but I for one hope not. Down that road the city becomes a real Babel, a place where values sit uneasily alongside each other, best not spoken of or celebrated in public, in case someone is offended. To avoid hatred, the city is emptied of our loves, and becomes just a place for doing business — commercial, legal, administrative. Community shrivels to no more than a convenient framework for the pursuit of individual goals.

But we need shared loves and ideals: where there is no vision, says the book of Proverbs, the people perish. The crowds who thunder out Blake's Jerusalem at the Proms every year, or before big football matches, are doing more than just singing a rousing song: we all yearn for our world to be just that bit more like the holy city of the vision:

> I will not cease from mental fight,
> nor shall my sword sleep in my hand,
> till we have built Jerusalem
> in England's green and pleasant land.

It's a noble and necessary longing. No city worth its salt can be built on the avoidance of common value. We need to celebrate and nourish the sense that this place we live our lives in isn't just somewhere to buy and sell, but a community in which we can share ideals and commitments. That conviction is expressed in the layout of every decent city from ancient Greece to modern Cambridge. They are all built round the market-place, certainly, but equally round the law court and the temple — in our case Market Hill, the Guildhall and Great St Mary's and this church.

And the faith embodied in these churches goes on having something to say even to the secular city. Today is Trinity Sunday, and this church is dedicated to the mystery of the Holy Trinity. Clergy sometimes treat sermons about the Trinity as an unpleasant and difficult annual chore. In general we shy away from talking about the Trinity, as if it were some irrelevant conundrum, an abstract piece of celestial mathematics which we need do no more than pay lip service to. In fact, the mystery of the Trinity is the heart of what Christianity has to say to the world. Our deepest and truest identity, as individuals and as members of communities, comes from sharing the life of God: we are only real and alive, to the extent that we share that divine life. And the doctrine of the Trinity tells us that God is not some immense cosmic individual, a lonely power before whom we must bow down and adore. The innermost being and reality of God which we are called to share is not isolation, but relationship: God is love.

And that means that we ourselves are not individuals first and foremost, and only then, and secondarily, members of a community. Mrs Thatcher, notoriously, once said that there was no such thing as society. The Christian proclamation of the Trinity insists that there is nothing else *except* society. We become people only in relation to others: our minds form and become *our* minds, us, not in isolation, but through interaction with others, as we acquire and use language. In the beginning was the Word. We learn who we are in relating to others. So our deepest reality and our deepest worth is not what we are in isolation, but what we are together with others. We are citizens as soon as we are people. We are made for each other, we were redeemed at great cost by the selfless outpouring of divine love.

Our city must reflect that reality. We must learn to live alongside each other not by avoiding speaking of our loves, but by listening to each other's loves. We don't need less faith in the city, we need more of it: more faith, more hope, more love, more idealism, more forgiveness, more concern for each other, more eagerness to welcome and care for the fragile and the unlovely, more attention to whatsoever things are true, honest, just, pure, lovely, and of good report.

Christianity, thank God, no longer has the power to force others, and it no longer has a monopoly on the values of society. Other faiths, other hopes, other loves, inform and shape our communities. But at the heart of the city, the Church can and must go on offering that witness about human nature and human community, rooted in the reality of God, grounded in love. It is a witness which the world and the city needs.

15

Light in the darkness

Monastic Vespers, Magdalene College,
Cambridge, 2000

Above the entrance to every staircase in First Court, there is
a stone shield with a coat of arms, painted and gilded and
venerable looking, one of the many reminders round the
College that we belong to an ancient foundation with a long
history. These shields, as you probably know, carry the arms
of four great medieval Benedictine monasteries of East
Anglia – Ely, Ramsey, Walden and Crowland – all of which
sent monks here to take degrees in the fifteenth and early
sixteenth centuries. But like so many Cambridge reminders
of the past, they are in fact more than a little bogus: despite
their pleasantly dilapidated appearance, they were in fact put
there as recently as 1928, a belated part of the antiquarian
recovery of the College's history which A.C. Benson did so
much to initiate and pay for. So, sadly, the shields are not so
much history as heritage, less a genuine mark of continuity
than a decorative allusion to a remote past, from which the
College has long since been safely disconnected.

The same could be said, you might be forgiven for
thinking, about the service we have just celebrated. There

is, of course, something haunting about the solemn sim-
plicity of Latin Vespers sung here in this former monastic
chapel by the monks of the modern-day equivalent of
medieval Magdalene, Benet Hall in Oxford. But it might
be nothing more than heritage, a nostalgic sacred concert,
something to tell your friends about, and just the thing to
get you into the right frame of mind for a candlelit dinner
in Hall. Plainsong, I gather, is all the rage these days, and
even the monks themselves are cashing in on it: Downside
and Ampleforth have entered the boom market established
by the monks of Silos in Spain, and have made bestselling
records with titles like *Gregorian Moods*. My teenage
daughter tells me that the organisers of raves and rock
concerts sometimes end the night's proceedings by playing
ten minutes or so of these CDs of plainsong, because it is
ideal for calming everybody down.

And there you have it: religion Classic-FM style,
soothing wallpaper. Never mind the meaning, get hold of
the sensation. A monk at a monastery which has recently
made two very successful records told me that the
designers of their CD sleeves had insisted that, while it
would be all right to have a suitably romantic gothic arch
or even the robed figure of a monk on the sleeve, they
must on no account include any overtly Christian symbol,
such as a cross or the name of Christ. Monks were OK,
even funky – after all, there are Buddhist monks, aren't
there – but hard religion was definitely a turn-off for the
CD-buying public.

So there's an uncomfortable discrepancy here, which
gets worse if you look in detail at the shields over the

doors into the Porter's Lodge and the College bar. They
are both versions of the shield of Crowland Abbey, and
they bristle with signs of severity: butcher's knives and
scourges made of knotted ropes. Crowland was our
mother house: the Abbots of Crowland paid for the
buildings in First Court, and the prior of the medieval
monk's hostel was always a Crowland monk. Crowland
claimed to be built over the bones of the great Anglo-
Saxon Fenland hermit, St Guthlac. The scourge on our
shield is his scourge; the butcher's knife the symbol of his
patron saint, the Apostle Bartholomew, on whose feast-
day he first settled at Crowland, and who in fact gave him
the scourge in a vision to fend off the demons that
swarmed in what was then the most desolate desert in
England, the impenetrable fenland of bog and black water
which spread from Cambridge to the Humber.

The knives and scourges, then, describe an ancient and
sobering reality. Guthlac's religion was craggy, uncomfortable and uncompromising, unimaginably different
from ours: he came to the wilderness of Crowland as a
refugee twice over from the company of other men. At
the age of twenty-six he had suddenly abandoned a career
as a successful and blood-thirsty Mercian warlord, in
favour of life in the monastery of Repton. In his two years
at Repton he acquired the essential tool of the Anglo-
Saxon monk – the ability to recite from memory all 150
psalms in Latin – but he antagonized even his monastic
brethren by his spectacular and competetive asceticism.
He had come to monastic life driven by an overwhelming
sense of the transience and darkness of human existence. It

was a common enough theme in Anglo-Saxon Christianity — there's a famous passage in Bede's *Ecclesiastical History of the English People*, in which one of the counsellors of King Edwin of Northumbria makes a comparison between the life of a man and the fleeting passage of a sparrow through a firelit banqueting hall in winter:

Inside all is warm, while outside the wintry storms of rain and snow are raging: the sparrow enters in at one door and quickly flies out through the other. For the few moments it is inside, the storm and wintry tempest cannot touch it, but after the briefest moment of calm, it flits from your sight, out of the wintry storm and into it again. So this life of man appears for a moment, what follows or indeed what went before we know nothing of at all. If this new doctrine of Christ brings us more information, it seems right that we should embrace it.

For Bede and his contemporaries, the storm and darkness were not just the great unknown before birth and after death, they surrounded every human life through all its phases. Guthlac's biographer tells us that the saint abandoned warfare because he found himself 'storm-tossed amid the gloomy clouds of life's darkness and amid the whirling waves of the world'. He found no refuge from those storms within the monastery, however, and eventually he sought out the most desolate region in the England of his day, a watery desert haunted by nameless terrors and demons, where others had tried and failed to live a hermit's life. He was a man self-consciously cast in the heroic role of dragon-slayer, setting out into a desert beyond human company or human help to wrestle, as Beowulf fought with Grendel, with the internal demons of his own sinfulness, and with those equally terrifying external demons whom Guthlac and his contemporaries believed haunted the wastes of the fen. The scourge which Bartholomew gave him was a symbol of the renunciation of comfort and pleasure, the embrace of penance and watchfulness, which would enable him to overcome his inner and outer demons.

And that much at least was meant to be perpetuated in the monastery that was eventually founded in the seat of his hermitage. The first monks, like Guthlac, were convinced that, like Christ, they fled into the desert not to run away from temptation, but to encounter it in its strongholds: the demons, they knew, were to be met everywhere, and most dangerously of all when the veneer of normality was removed, and men and women were left alone with their thoughts, with the time and the clarity of vision to see things, and themselves, as they really are. Monastic buildings were raised as signposts of transcendence, a summons away from spiritual mediocrity and a call to something more absolute and demanding: to honesty and self-knowledge.

At any rate, that was the theory. In practice, of course, monasteries often were and are something less. Monks cannot marry, but in the Middle Ages they ate more regularly and slept warmer than most of their contemporaries, and they were cushioned against the precariousness of everyday life by their membership of a great landed institution, whose Abbot was one of the most powerful men in the realm, a lord of Parliament and the ruler of estates which ran the breadth of eastern England.

So by the time that the monks of Crowland came to build this place, monasticism had long since ceased to mean what Guthlac had meant by it. Go to the Monk's room, or the Captain of Boats room, where the framework and some of the detail of the monastic buildings established here by Abbot John de Wisbech are still visible, and look at the ceiling beams: by fifteenth-century standards they were, quite simply, plush; the staircases of First Court were the richest and best College buildings in the Cambridge of their day, luxury lodgings for men who did not relish hardship.

If monasticism was all about asceticism and world renunciation then we would all of us, monks and secular men and women, have a good deal to feel uncomfortable about tonight, as we measure the distance between symbol and reality.

But in fact tonight's service inserts us into another equally crucial aspect of monastic life from which we are not so far removed, even in Cambridge, even in Magdalene. Benedictine monasticism has never laid much stress on extreme asceticism: instead it has offered the world a vision of a communal life ordered towards eternity in a regular rhythm of prayer, work and study. Above all the monk is dedicated to the *opus dei*, the praise of God which is an integral part of the contemplative life. And part and parcel of that work of God is *Lectio Divina*, the slow, attentive, ruminative encounter with the Word of God which is designed to permeate and shape the whole of life and all our values and attitudes.

And whether or not we are believers, that sacred reading and internalization of the Word of God is in fact the model for the work *we* do here in the University. In so far as they are honest explorations of reality, *all* forms of study are forms of contemplativity, even forms of prayer. The medieval Universities emerged out of the monastic and cathedral schools, and the western ideal of study – the attentive observation of a world for its own sake, and not just as something to be managed or exploited or sold or eaten – was shaped by the doctrine of creation. If we believe that the world issues from the hand of God – even more, if we believe that the eternal Logos, Divine intelligence himself, took flesh within his creation, if we believe that he learned with a human mind and hoped and loved with a human heart; then the study of everything created, the whole material order from the tiniest molecule to the most remote galaxy, from the use of the aorist tense to the poetics of Aristotle, becomes an act of homage to and faith in the creator.

That is why medieval monks thought everything worth studying, and why it was in the medieval monasteries that the remnants of pagan learning, even the obscene or secular poetries of Catullus or Horace, were copied and preserved. When we attempt to make sense of anything at all, and to utter the sense we have made, we imitate the creating Word of God himself, and we celebrate the order and coherence of the world which that Word has called into being. In that sense, every scientific theory, every mathematical formula, every historical paper, is a liturgical text, and the chanting of the Psalms merely makes explicit the fundamental celebration of meaning and coherence without which we would hardly be human at all.

But of course there is more to it than that: we should not forget the darkness outside and within us, we should not forget Guthlac's demons. We are not simply delighted observers of the spectacle of creation: we are part of creation, flotsam on the stream of time, ourselves caught up in the flow of energies which make up the material world. We experience power, life and growth in the cell under the microscope, in the sunrise, in the trees along the Backs: but we suffer them also in the earthquake or in the terrible vigour of a cancer. Our dignity and our burden is to be that part of creation which is conscious not only of itself but of its finitude. We alone of all created things have taken the measure of mortality, we alone of all the creatures know that we are dying. We sing to the light in the midst of a darkness which we know will one day devour us.

And so this evening celebration of the monastic *opus dei* is not confined to praise: it reminds us that the Divine Word entered his world and became a man not merely to live, but to die; not simply as the culminating act of creation, but, by sharing our lot, to heal and comfort and assure us that the light is stronger than the dark, that despite all signs to the contrary, suffering and chaos and death are not God's final words to the world. We can credit that world, we can put our trust in the possibility of meaning, because we believe it has been both created and redeemed. It comes from God, and, beyond all its unimaginable and sublime complexities, it will find its end in him.

Nowadays, the University is inexorably being colonized by the values of the marketplace. Research is market-led, funding is given to work with direct commercial application, and learning is valued by whether or not it can be sold. In candlelit Chapel and candlelit Hall tonight it is good to be reminded of the real meaning of our University: that we are not a shop or a factory, but a community of human beings who share a common life, so that we can support one another in our efforts to make sense of the whole of this terrible and wonderful world – the world God made, and shed his blood for.

16

The God of History

Magdalene College Chapel
Readings: Gen. 38; Mt 1:1–17.

You may remember the row in the press a few years ago
over the proposed sale of the Hereford *Mappa Mundi*, a
unique medieval map of the world which the Dean and
Chapter proposed to flog to the highest bidder. One of the
many letters to the newspapers on the subject asked what
all the fuss was about, since in the writer's view it was
rather a silly map, with important places like England
squeezed into a corner, and with Jerusalem set fair and
square in the centre. Whoever drew it was a rotten
geographer.

Geography, of course, was not the point. The maker of
the *Mappa Mundi* was making a theological claim of the
centrality of the city of Jerusalem, and therefore of the
people of Israel, in the history of humanity. Jerusalem was
at the centre of the world because Christ had died there.
The map was drawn that way because God is the God of a
people – he is the God of History.

What sort of a God is that, and do we believe in him?
Clearly, Christians *once* did so: at the centre of the Creed

we recited earlier this evening there is a *date*. Jesus died *sub Pontio Pilato*, 'under Pontius Pilate'. That date was once believed to be the pivot of history, as Jerusalem was the centre of the world. The world began four thousand years before Christ, and from the beginning of the world to the birth – and death – of Jesus, history unfolded itself according to God's plan, converging inexorably on that time, that place. After it, history moved, and moves, towards its consummation at the end of time. And the meaning of all history was to be found in the story of Jesus: time was measured by the ideas of years before and years after his birth. It was all very clear cut and reassuring.

But that sharply-focussed picture began to blur almost as soon as Europe began to take seriously the existence of other cultures and races, other histories, other civilizations, other religions. If Jesus and Jesus' ancestors were the centre of human history, wasn't all the rest of human history a massive irrelevance? All very well to see our Jewish-Christian tradition as the key to it all, Jerusalem as the centre of the world; but there seemed an awful lot of locks that the key didn't fit. What of all the tens and hundreds of millions of people who were born and lived and died without ever so much as hearing of Jesus? Was God the God of their history too?

It's a question Christians and unbelievers alike have been asking ever since the days of St Augustine, with gathering urgency; and it is still one of the most crucial of all theological questions. In our age it has taken on a new dimension, for it is not only the *God* of History that seems hard to believe in, but the idea of history itself. We live in a world of events, not of history, our lives structured not by some grand narrative, but by the cascade of anecdote and rumour and fact that pours out at us from the media. Few people in our society see themselves as part of some great story unfolding itself purposefully. Night after night we watch on television event after event. A political scandal here, a kidnapping there, a strike yesterday, a war or an air disaster today: the only connection between them the voyeuristic eye of the television, *our* eye, pausing momentarily to watch a child die of malnutrition, or a goal scored, before moving on, the last item forgotten already as the new picture flashes upon us. And for many of us, even for believers, it seems our lives themselves are lived like a news programme, not a story with an overall meaning and direction, but a random sequence, one damn thing after another.

That is, I, think, a fair reflection of what our culture, our world, is increasingly like – disjointed, random, without agreed structure or coherence. And in such a world the grand biblical narrative, the sweep of God's purpose from Eden to Egypt, from Egypt to Canaan, from Canaan to Calvary, from Calvary to Armageddon, seems alien. The biblical certainty that everything adds up, that all events are part of one story, seems too glib, and we are suspicious of it. Behind the voice of the man who knows what it's all about, who can explain the direction of the march of history, it's all too easy to catch the tramp-tramp-tramp of the jackboot, the relentless harangue of some over-certain ayatollah intent on Jihad. As W.B. Yeats wrote,

The best lack all conviction, and the worst
Are full of passionate intensity.

In fact, the biblical view of God's action in the world
doesn't offer such majestic certainties, and the Bible again
and again reminds us that, if the human trek through time
has meaning, it is *not* as part of some relentless grand plan,
moving towards some thousand-year Reich. If Jesus died
sub Pontio Pilato, at an identifiable place, on a certain day,
under a datable emperor, he died unnoticed by all except
his disciples, in an obscure province, not at the centre but
at the edge of the world; and his living and dying seemed
not even a footnote in the real history of humanity. His
life had all the same apparent inconsequentiality as ours.

And that same apparent inconsequentiality, I think, has
something to do with the power of the story we heard
read earlier in the service, the story of Tamaar and Judah.
Its sordidness seems the very stuff of tabloid newspapers.
Deceit, promise-breaking, the victimization of the weak,
incest: it's like an episode of *EastEnders*, or a lead story in
the *Sun*. This is history as we have come to think of it:
sensational, grubby, and non-directional.

It has always been a problem story. Whoever stitched
together the collection of tales which we now call the
Book of Genesis couldn't find anywhere sensible to put it.
Pushed into its present position, between chapters 37 and
39, it is clearly out of place, breaking up the sweep and
symmetry of the Joseph story, yet just too important to be
left out. It's easy to see why, because this is surely one of
the most vivid and satisfying stories in the Old Testament

(and indeed in the whole of ancient literature) not least because, unlike the Exodus or the prophecies of Isaiah or the Apocalypse, it reveals to us the world as we experience it – shapeless, messy, and grim.

It's worth looking at the details. Judah marries a foreign wife and has three sons: Er, Onan, Shelah. The eldest, Er, also takes a foreign wife, Tamar, but Er is no good, and God removes him from the scene before they get round to having a family. In ancient Israel it was a terrible thing for a man to die without children, and under Israel's law, a widow in such circumstances was entitled to marry one of her husband's relatives; the first child of this marriage would then be counted as the offspring of the first husband. In terms of the pastoral society for which it was conceived, it was a compassionate and just law – it ensured the secure transmission of the family's name and property, provided for the widow, and took away from her the reproach of childlessness. And so the second son, Onan, duly marries Tamar. But the Bar-Judahs are not a nice or a close-knit family. Onan has no love for his dead brother, and though he sleeps with his new wife, he practises *coitus interuptus* so that there shall be no child to his brother's name. God is enraged by his cynicism, and Onan too dies.

By now, Judah is becoming alarmed. To lose one husband may be considered a misfortune: to lose two looks like carelessness. Tamar has a right to marry the third son, Shelah, but Judah is determined that she won't, and he plays for time: 'The boy's a bit young, go home to your parents, later we'll have a wedding.' Tamar is not fooled: she knows Judah intends to cheat her, and she determines to outwit him. On hearing that he's about to move up-country with his herds, she disguises herself in the veil of one of the cultic prostitutes who were commonly found near shrines in ancient Israel. She is evidently a shrewd girl, and has spotted her father-in-law's weakness. Judah can't resist a pretty veil, and he kerb-crawls over and asks her price. She demands a young goat, and when he points put that he doesn't have one on him, she says that the Ancient Israelite equivalent of American Express will do nicely: she asks for his signet, bracelet and staff as security. The deal is struck, and he goes to bed with her. Judah is evidently a better man than any of his sons, and Tamar immediately becomes pregnant. Exultant, she goes back home, sheds her disguise, and settles down to wait.

And in due course news reaches Judah that his daughter-in-law, supposedly in decorous retirement as a childless widow, has been no better than she ought to be, and is pregnant. He's not an imaginative man, and clearly hadn't paused to remove the harlot's veil when he visited her tent on his way north, so the devastating irony of the announcement that she has been 'playing the harlot' is lost on him: but here is a golden opportunity to get this unlucky girl out of the family. He seizes it.

Judah is Everyman, decent enough when it doesn't hurt. In the previous chapter it's he who persuades the rest of his brothers not to kill Joseph – 'Let's just sell him into slavery.' But as that suggests, he's more concerned with appearances than with righteousness: and so it proves now. 'Let her be burned,' he insists. Behind his vehemence we hear at once relief that he can rid himself of this unlucky girl, and submerged guilt at the knowledge that he has cheated her of her rights in preventing her marrying the third son. And now the tables are turned. Tamar sends Judah the pledges he gave the prostitute. He is confronted with his own actions, and the knowledge that his daughter-in-law has seen through him, and has accomplished the law despite him. And Judah acknowledged them and said, 'She has been more righteous than I.'

It's a sordid story, in which everyone is tricking someone else, and in which even Tamar, who *is* concerned with righteousness, only achieves it by exploiting Judah's weak spot, his lust. Envy, treachery, lies and lust: with a lesser storyteller, or a more naïve and optimistic theology, the story might have ended there, but in fact it has a bitter little coda: Tamar has not one son in her womb, but two. These children have been conceived in a thug's world of cheating, lies, and exploitation, and they are worthy of the world that has made them: the last glimpse we get of them is in a struggle for dominance within the womb itself, as they wrestle over who shall be born first, for in this world, winner takes all.

It's an astonishingly subversive story. It's not my theme now, but reflect on its implications for an understanding of the place of women in Israel. At the obvious level you couldn't have a more passive role for a woman, handed on from man to man, her very life at the disposal of the male head of her husband's family. And when Tamar at last takes the law into her own hands, it is in the character of that most abject symbol of man's exploitation of woman, a prostitute. And yet, it is precisely this oppressed and passive creature, Tamar, who is the central figure in the story, the real agent who, against all the odds, brings about the righteousness that Judah has tried to cheat. As so often in the Old Testament, the conscious attitude of Israel towards women is undercut and turned on its head by the hidden dynamism of the story and the God who works behind it, that God who puts down the mighty from their thrones and raises up the humble and meek.

Odder still, or at least more obvious, is the apparent *absence* of that God from the story. He makes two brief appearances, but only to clear Er and Onan out of the way: the story is not *about* God – or rather, it is about the fact that God's purpose is always hidden in the apparent purposelessness of human nature. His is the *Tsedek*, the righteousness, which a reluctant Judah is brought to acknowledge, for Israel's God, our God, is the Father of the widow and the orphan. But the dimensions of his righteousness are revealed in all the sordidness and trickery and half-truths of human action. There is no revelation, no grand plan, no supernatural intervention. And yet there is judgement, and repentance, and recognition. The God of this story is God incarnate, immanent in the all too sullied flesh of weak men and women, powerful to bring his ends out of the slyness and evasions of even the worst human behaviour.

And that is why the sordid circle of this circle is not closed, is not a circle at all. That is why, when Matthew came to write his Gospel, he went to considerable trouble in the opening lines to draw our attention to this extraordinary story. For Judah and Tamar and their child

Pharez are the ancestors of Jesus. The genealogy of Jesus in St Matthew's Gospel is a male one: it recites the names of Jesus' male ancestors from Abraham to Joseph. But Matthew does mention just five women in the course of this catalogue of male names, and Tamar is the first of them. The baby who emerged first from her womb after a struggle with his brother was Phares, and he was the ancestor of Jesus.

The other women Matthew mentions are Rahab, Ruth, Bathsheba, and Mary. These are carefully selected names, for like Tamar, all these women were sexually compromised. Rahab was a sort of Mata Hari figure, a prostitute who collaborated with the first Israelite spies into the Holy Land, and let them into the city of Jericho so that they could slaughter all the inhabitants. Ruth, like Tamar, was a vulnerable woman left without protection in a man's world, and, in the manner of Tamar, tricked her kinsman Boaz into marrying her by getting into his bed and surprising him when he woke up in the morning. Bathsheba was spied on by King David while she bathed naked on her roof one hot summer's evening, and married him after he had murdered her husband. And Mary, like Tamar, was suspected by Joseph of having played the harlot by getting pregnant without the help of a husband. These are the ancestresses whom Matthew has given to Jesus. From this contaminated stream is drawn the pure abounding water of life. Matthew here confronts us with God's inversion of our values, with God's refusal to be confined within the bounds of the likely or the respectable. The Christ who sat down and ate with harlots and sinners is consistent from his very beginning.

By pointing at the beginning of his Gospel to Tamar, Matthew is letting us know what sort of God we have, what sort of a thing the Incarnation is. 'God with us' means just that. The grace and truth and righteousness we recognize in Jesus, we must learn to recognize *outside* the safe world of the nice and the good, *outside* the charmed circle of religion. God's truth and power are elusive, liable to be pushed into the dark corners of our lives and our society. We need to recognize and respond to his presence in the actual, not the *ideal* world of men and women, a world which he has made and loves, and in every corner of which he dwells. But if the story of Tamar is any clue, we should not expect the righteousness of God to be blindingly apparent, nor his religion a textbook to life with the answers neatly printed at the foot of the page. The moral majority and all the confidant purveyors of agony- and doubt-free existence have no place in Tamar's world, which is the world into which Christ was born and for which he died. We will find the righteousness of God revealed and vindicated where we most need it, in the ambivalent and often murky encounter with those we love, but never enough; in the society of duplicity and partial justice which is all even the best of us really aspires to.

But if that means that we can't expect God's presence in the world to be obvious and apparent, it also means that there is nowhere we are not to look for it. It's one of the paradoxes of British life that the very same politicians who condemn the Churches for their lily-livered liberalism, and their failure to insist on traditional moral values, particularly respect for property, often want to insist that there are huge areas of our common life where moral and religious values have no meaning. The idea that economics or defence are areas in which different rules apply, and God is absent, where market forces or the balance of terror have to be given free reign, was one of the pillars of Thatcherism, and politicians regularly tell Christian leaders to mind their own business and concentrate on religious matters, leaving secular issues of economics and political stategy to those who know. The story of Tamar reveals to us that this is in fact a trick to baffle God's righteousness, to exclude it from the fabric of our daily lives. But that righteousness, hidden and obscure as it may be, is at work everywhere that human evil seeks to frustrate it, and everywhere that human need evokes its mercy. There is nothing outside its scope, no aspect of the common life of men and women in which it cannot and will not manifest itself. Painful and puzzling as the process may be, we must seek to uncover God's will and God's work even in unpromising places like the City or the Cabinet room. We are not allowed to confine God to the safe boundaries of religion, nor to escape into the safety of religion from His questioning, startling presence in our murky and irreligious lives. For God has not gathered us into His masterplan. Instead, he himself has entered into our cluelessness: he is close at hand, however we seek to evade him, he will show us what we are. For the Word became flesh, and dwells amongst us.